"If anyone is qua~~lified to write this~~ ... who has heard and felt the grief of many during his thirty years as a counselor, apart from experiencing personal tragedy himself. This book shows you how not to succumb to tragedy but to supersede it and rebuild your life."—**Arun Gandhi**, founder/president, M. K. Gandhi Institute for Nonviolence

"There are so many good and remarkable gifts in this honest telling of love and loss. But I think the finest is the transition Hal Edwards lets us witness as he moves from cherished conversations with his wife, Betsy, when she was still alive, to a continuing conversation with her spirit after her death, and ultimately his sense of connection with all that is. In his words, 'There will be a significant calm and deep trust as you take life as it comes to you. . . . You will find yourself existing in a growing awareness of Divine Love fully operative within your being, regardless of circumstances.'"
—**Paula D'Arcy**, author, *Gift of the Red Bird* and *Winter of the Heart*

"For 28 years I had the privilege of sharing a small support group with Hal Edwards. Hal's book is my companion now as we work through the inevitabilities of my wife's aphasia. Hal's honesty probes in ways doctors do at times to find out where it hurts, name it, and face it. We are understanding how to celebrate the vulnerability of each little diminishment."—**Rev. Ray Bakke, Ph.D.**, author, *A Theology as Big as a City*

"Whatever our loss, we do not want to get stuck in the process; the result would be devastating! This book by Hal Edwards helps us remember that there is no grief we cannot survive and grow through."—**Fr. Patrick Keith Hosey**, former director of John XXIII Retreat Center, Hartford City, Indiana

"Jesus taught us, in Matthew 5:4, *Blessed are those who mourn, for they shall be comforted*. Facing my own mortality through cancer again, I have been comforted by others who have experienced loss with fearless grace. It is an honor to have my endorsement included in this much-needed book because it seems ridiculous in a culture like ours, so focused on diversions and entertainment, that crying is a stumbling block to men. We must teach all young people to cry. Hal's book companions us on our journey through grief into joyful gratitude."
—**Fr. Richard Rohr, OFM,** director of the Center for Action and Contemplation, author, *The Universal Christ* and *Falling Upward*

"Hal Edwards poignantly and courageously chronicles his vulner-abilities, challenges, and opportunities in grieving through the greatest loss of his life. With candor and humility, he traces how the profound sense of loss alters his life and how new pathways had to be found to 'get on with his life.' Readers are not only reminded that each of us has the value and power to move beyond the prism of grief, but Hal Edwards provides practices to do so. In a myriad of ways, his book says to me, *Honor your grief . . . for therein lies your soul*."
—**Dolores E. Cross, Ph.D.,** retired professor and college president

"While working the story arc of Hal's meaningful and powerful book, I experienced the death of my mother and my father. Hal's wisdom and courageous vulnerability delivered in words the map, permission, and comfort my own grief craved. Grief *is* the great change agent. Hal's integrity with grief teaches us all how to let death heal."—**Megan Wells, MFA,** master storyteller and coach

"Know that as you read Hal's book my thoughts and prayers are with you in your time of mourning. Having traveled a similar journey as you, be assured that, in the fullness of time, all will be well."—**Howard Morgan,** former senior vice president of Citibank, Chicago

"*Grief's Journey* is a *profound* and yet *practical* companion for those times of great loss that come to all of us—especially as we move into the second half of life. Sensitively and honestly, Hal Edwards writes of the 'larger life' that came to him heralded by grief over the loss of his beloved wife, Betsy. I have known Hal and Betsy since the 1970s. I witnessed their integrity. I trust Hal as he gently points the way to invite the love gifts of grief or 'disguised grace,' into our lives and assures us that they are always available in every circumstance."
**—Paula Payne Hardin, Ed.D., MPS**, author *What Are You Doing with the Rest of Your Life?*

"I love this book! Hal Edwards takes us along on his walk with grief over the loss of his beloved wife. He shares the tender details of what he experienced in the days, weeks, and months after her death. His grief was searing, yet it also matured and grounded his already-deep spiritual life. This book is a treasure trove of help for grievers, especially the sections on the benefits of journaling, community, prayer, dreamwork, and paranormal experiences. I will read it again and again, not just when grieving, but also to deepen my living now. It is a truly wonderful book."—**Dr. Kay Metres**, author, *After the Fear Come the Gifts*

"Having spent forty years as a cancer surgeon, I have witnessed countless responses to those experiencing a loved one's death. I felt Hal's words take my hand and bring me into his experience where tears of empathy over his loss led me into insight and wisdom accompanied by silent "aha" moments. This work is a roadmap that offers guidance to help the mourner not only survive but actually spiritually grow. *Grief's Journey* is a worthy companion to those in mourning. When the next major loss in my life occurs, I know I will turn to this book for guidance, solace, and growth."
**—Thomas R. Witt, MD**, retired surgeon, Rush University Medical Center, Chicago

"*Grief's Journey* is a narrative that will enhance Pastoral Care both within and beyond local assemblies as well as academic communities. Hal has captured Rabbi Maimonides' concept of the 'middle path,' showing us how to seek harmony and grow into internal healing and peace while experiencing grief as a difficult experience, yet one that can be empowering and not impossible to overcome."—**Rev. B Herbert Martin**, pastor emeritus, Progressive Community Church

"Hal Edwards' book on the grieving process has left me marveling at how profound that process is in our own transformation as we muddle our way through it. The taking time and the paying attention to our inner world during that process somehow allow grief's work to restore wholeness and completion. Gratitude abounds for Hal's meticulous sharing of his own journey through grieving."
—**Patricia L. Johnson**, administrator of Intensive Retreats at St. Benedict's Monastery, Snowmass, Colorado

"Hal Edwards' moving and personal account of his journey with grief after the loss of his beloved wife, Betsy, is rich with insights and lessons he has learned along the way. With grief as his teacher, and as a wise and seasoned companion, he offers his experience and practical guidance to all who have had to bear the pain of loss—not only of loved ones, but other losses that life sets before us. Born of grief, this book will be a blessing to many."—**Frank T. Griswold**, 25th Presiding Bishop of the Episcopal Church

"The book is amazing! I loved reading every page and feel more prepared to deal with life's losses. The only certain thing in life is that it will end soon. In his *Grief's Journey*, Hal offers us tools to carve our path with divine possibilities, to not only deal with death but live in grace, gratitude, and happiness every moment through daily prayer, journaling, and communion."—**Hema Pokharna, PhD**, Interfaith Peacmaker and Mediator

"Hal's tender narrative of his wife's death is a powerful invitation for us to enter our own internal journeys. I lived with this book. I wept with this book. I laughed with this book. Affirming that each grief journey is unique, we nevertheless find ourselves engaging with the universal gift of grief through connection and practice. Hal's vulnerable and honest presence enables us to feel his companionship as we receive the gift that grief freely offers."—**Rev. Jolene Bergstrom Carlson**, retired pastor, spiritual director, Austin, Texas

"Fr. Thomas Keating said to Hal, 'Men don't know how to grieve,' but I think a lot of women don't either. This book is gutsy and courageous, and many men and women will benefit. What an evocative gift Hal Edwards shares with us, as he allows his life experience to be a wisdom teacher, so that we don't shrink, embitter, numb, or isolate ourselves from life! With graphic honesty and humility, Hal opens doors within us, like a good friend holding our hand as we walk through empty darkness, so we don't collapse into flight or fight, but rather learn grief's lessons of trust, nonattachment, and freedom. It is a hard book to put down, so riveting are his companioning insights."—**Fr. Bob Colaresi, O.Carm.**, Carmelite Center, Illinois M.A.L.E.s

"Some models say that grief comes in stages. Mostly, grieving comes in waves. Sometimes the waves are shallow and gently splash at our being. At other times, the waves come in deep and bowl us over. As a board certified chaplain, licensed clinical professional counselor, spiritual director, and certified clinical pastoral educator, I have companioned many people through their grieving processes. Each person grieves uniquely. They make choices along the way. Some face loss and grief as if it is something 'out there' with denial and suppressed emotions as they rush 'to get over it.' Others, like Hal, face their loss and grief as lived experience in the depths of their souls.

Hal's story is true. I witnessed Hal experience his grieving process with integrity and a desire to grow. He entered a brave space and he did the inner work necessary to open himself to whole-hearted living in the midst of and beyond his sorrow and suffering. Hal's wisdom was hard won. In this book, he graciously offers to companion others on their unique grieving journeys and he invites them to find their true selves along the way."—**Rev. Ida-Regina Lucas Oliver, MEd, MA, M.Div., LCPC, BCC, ACPE**

"Having experienced, and witnessed, in our criminal courts indiscribable pain and suffering caused by losing a loved one, one cannot avoid wondering whether the pain ever goes away. This book gives guidelines, based on first-hand experience and profound spiritual guidance, that point the reader toward acceptance and moving on, while embracing the life-giving realities of those we have lost deep in our hearts."—**Judge Consuelo Bedoya**, retired Cook County Circuit Court, Chicago, Illinois

# GRIEF'S JOURNEY

*A Companion for Friends Who Mourn*

## HAL L. EDWARDS

LANTERN BOOKS • NEW YORK

*A Division of Booklight Inc.*

2019
Lantern Books
128 Second Place
Brooklyn, NY 11231
www.lanternbooks.com

Copyright © 2019 Hal L. Edwards

All rights reserved. No part of this book may be reproduced, stored in a retrieval system, or transmitted in any form or by any means, electronic, mechanical, photocopying, recording, or otherwise, without the written permission of Lantern Books.

Photo of Hal L. Edwards by Alan M. Levin

Printed in the United States of America

Names: Edwards, Hal, author.
Title: Grief's journey : a companion for friends who mourn / Hal Edwards.
Description: Brooklyn, NY : Lantern Books, [2019] | Includes bibliographical references.
Identifiers: LCCN 2019009844 (print) | LCCN 2019018497 (ebook) | ISBN 9781590565919 (ebook) | ISBN 9781590565902 (pbk. : alk. paper)
Subjects: LCSH: Grief. | Bereavement. | Loss (Psychology)
Classification: LCC BF575.G7 (ebook) | LCC BF575.G7 E29 2019 (print) | DDC 155.9/37—dc23
LC record available at https://lccn.loc.gov/2019009844

To Betsy

*I love thee with the breath,*
*Smiles, tears, of all my life; and, if God choose,*
*I shall but love thee better after death.*
—**Elizabeth Barrett Browning** (1806–1861), from *Sonnet 43*

# Contents

# Foreword

Hal Edwards' wife, Betsy, was a person of great prayer and mature character, warm, and full of charity towards others and a deep wisdom. Just to see her, and still more to meet her, was refreshing. In this book, Hal shares his profound grief in her sudden departure from this life. It shows how grief can be a transformative gift from God's love for humanity and its deeply wounded members. It embodies a process that moves from immense suffering at the loss of one's beloved into the emerging of a new relationship.

Although physical love-making has been taken away by death, the continuing spiritual presence to each other becomes—over time—a source of joy: one that is liberating, tender, sublime, and permanent. The pain of initial separation is swallowed up by a spiritual bond that is even more supportive than the physical and emotional bonding that is no more. It is impossible to go on grieving when the loss of your beloved is gradually replaced by an abiding happiness in the realization of a new relationship that never grows weary or diminishes.

The cost of this spiritual relationship with its permanent sense of union is the total acceptance of the initial pain of seemingly unbearable suffering. Hal reveals what this passage was for him with complete honesty and frankness. His book is a manual for grieving lovers. They will find their own moments of loneliness, piercing memories, and anguished emotions reflected with great force and realism.

Suffering accepted, or at least the effort to accept it, leads to profound insights into who God is and the reassurance of being united to him. It makes us one with God and with his compassion for all who suffer great personal loss.

Fr. Thomas Keating,
St. Benedict's Abbey
Snowmass, Colorado

# Introduction

This is my story about what I learned, grieving through the greatest loss of my life.

On a scorching Chicago day in July 2005, my wife Betsy and I spent the afternoon working in our backyard garden. The overbearing heat drove Betsy indoors to air conditioning and a short nap. As I was left alone to cultivate our beloved heirloom tomatoes, John, my former barber, came to mind. Haircut time was also our time to swap garden stories. One fateful day, just like that, John fell over in his tomato patch and died right there on the spot. Totally engrossed in this memory, visualizing John lying among his cherished tomatoes, I imagined my own inevitable diminishment. In solidarity with John I announced aloud to myself, "Wow! What a fantastic way to go!"

I dropped my trowel, ran into the house, kicked off my shoes, ran upstairs, slumped across our bed, looked straight into Betsy's bright blue eyes, and proclaimed, "*You* are gonna outlive me, woman! No doubt about it!"

"Nah, that's what you think!" she blurted back.

"Oh no! I'm going first. I'm not hanging around here without you!" I jabbed back.

"Not a chance. Don't think so," she refuted.

I countered, "I'm going out like John, just like that, in our tomato patch!"

We joshed back and forth, laughing until we were happily spent. Gazing deeply into each other's eyes, we treasured the delightful joy of mutual connection, basking in a moment of soulful wonderment.

I never doubted Betsy would outlive me; of course she would. Hadn't Mike, my financial advisor, quoted national insurance statistics confirming that women in general outlive men? I'd judiciously managed our financial portfolio since the mid-eighties with Mike's statistical mandate grounded in my mind. Betsy was equally resolute that I would outlive her.

Whenever we discussed retirement, we looked forward to spending many quality years together. Retirement would be our time to co-create precious down-to-earth memories and legacies. The following year, we eagerly sorted, discarded, packed, and gave away family heirlooms teeming with heartwarming memories.

A month later, we found our dream home in appropriately named Lake County, four houses from Bangs Lake, in Wauconda, which is the Native American word for "spirit waters."

I called my friend Nelson to help us procure a moving company. Always the joker, he said out of the side of his mouth, "Did you know that forty percent of people who move after seventy years of age die within six months?" We laughed. Another Nelson Irving joke, true to form. That year I was seventy-one and Betsy was seventy.

We moved on May 20, 2006. We imagined a new lifestyle—traveling, gardening, fishing, boating, swimming; enjoying family and friends over for outdoor barbeques. Our meditation group, fifteen years along, would continue to meet every week, in our family room.

*Exactly six months later paramedics arrived at our house and rushed Betsy to Good Shepherd Hospital.*

My final message from Betsy before they intubated her for transport from Good Shepherd to Northwestern Hospital was scribbled onto paper. A Darth Vader oxygen mask firmly in place, she wrote, "Everything going very slow." We gave each other an ET finger-to-finger "hug." I kissed her on the forehead, and said, "Darling, we have a date downtown and don't you dare miss it!"

Betsy nodded gently.

I followed the ambulance. Driving alone into the city, I fully anticipated she would survive the ordeal, though fierce emotions tossed me back and forth.

I emailed daily updates to relatives and friends; I imagined them as my connecting link. Their responses, calls, visits, questions, and supportive feedback became my trustworthy lifejacket. Emails, reflections, poems, letters, dialogues, dreams, and daily journal entries poured forth.

After a month on life support, Betsy died.

I collapsed inside what felt like a mythical time machine, pitching and whirling through a maze of the unwanted, unrehearsed, and unpredictable. Everything familiar and foreseeable gave way to disorientation. Seared by emotions too powerful to confront directly, I kept writing. Recording my experiences in my journal gave me a container, a discerning shield—a cutting edge through of naïve optimism or depression as I muddled through agonizing pain. Writing it out of my skin became a manageable way to survive the unbearable. Natalie Goldberg explains this in her book *Writing Down the Bones*: "Life is so rich, if you can write down the real details of the way things were and are, you hardly need anything else" (p. 53).

Still, the subtle and overwhelming onslaught of grief wore at me daily. I struggled for balance between my inner world and my outer world, wondering how a person could genuinely welcome grief and maintain any degree of functionality in the midst of ongoing daily responsibilities. *When will this end? Is it time to get on with my life?* Grieving the loss of Betsy was not allowing me to do the latter; grief was causing complete havoc with my sense of control.

Rather than "get on with it," or even "get through it," I felt an inner call to trust and "enter into it." There was little hope of resisting the experience anyway; grief had me by the scruff of my neck and was marshaling me across uncharted turf.

This moment of decision, this acceptance, changed me to my core. Grieving the loss of my beloved Betsy, more than any other suffering of my life, cut right through my resistances and refined my entire human experience.

After Betsy's death, I shared my experience with Fr. Thomas Keating. After listening thoughtfully, he said, "Hal, I hope you will write your story. So many men do not know how to grieve."

Keating's comment proved to be the lynchpin that kept me focused and committed to more than a decade of refinement and self-discovery. I am equally aware of wounded women, like my beloved deceased mother, who confided how it was near impossible to outgrow anger and grief.

More than twelve years have passed since Betsy's death as I complete this manuscript. I have come through my acute grief and listened to many share their unique stories. I have learned that we all "do" grief differently. My story will not be your story; every person's grief creates a unique and unrepeatable path. Never buy into the illusion that a person should or should not grieve in any specific way. I believe there are two saving factors in a grief experience that keep the wheels of growth on the road: the decision to remain true to one's deepest self *and* a commitment to open to all that grief teaches.

It is my hope that this book will assist you as you choose to trust the mysterious gift of your grief. I hope it will in some small way serve as a timely companion for your unique journey. I encourage you to keep a notebook or journal close by and write down your questions, notes, and reflections.

The format of this book has been divided into three parts:

Part I—Experience: What happened during the initial weeks and months before and after Betsy's death, including associations, flashbacks, and memories that surfaced during those intense times.

Part II—Practice: Practices, methods, and guidelines that proved their weight in gold during my grieving tenure.

Part III—Guide: Questions related to Part I are designed to help enliven your thoughts and feelings in personal reflection or in group sharing.

I recall the water in my grandmother's old Mason jar, sitting close by the hand pump on my childhood back porch. She emptied that jar of start-up water down the throat of the old hand pump, vigorously pumping the handle up and down until the start-up water created an airtight pipeline, suctioning fresh, pure well water up out of the hidden depths. I hope my story, like that quart of water, pulls up some of the hidden connections that await you deep in your psychic underground. If that happens, it would be the highest tribute you could bestow on our encounter.

## *Part I*

# EXPERIENCE

*Stone Portal* by Esterita Austin

Betsy's definitive project, this quilted wall hanging, memorializes her creative hand and articulates her final epiphany. Short of breath and lacking physical strength, she poured body and soul into the color and texture of this vibrant fabric of hallowed ancient stones infused with light and hope.

# A Surreal Moment in Real Time

"So I will disappear from view . . ."
**—Thomas Merton** (Higgins, p. 98)

We were in the Cardiac Care Unit at Northwestern Memorial Hospital in Chicago, Illinois. A month of vigil. Betsy lay unconscious in her bed, tubes attached to her body, her chest rising and falling at the will of the ventilator. Friends and relatives, an even dozen, were gathered for a pizza party, licking fingers juicy with Gino's East deep-dish pizza and salad. The hiss of the life-sustaining machinery, like beaching waves, persisted beneath the voices. Hospital staff came and left, briefly joining us for pizza and conversation.

I left the room for a restroom break, pausing for a moment to gaze at a now familiar painting on the hallway wall. The framed image of two mothers watching children chase gulls along the seashore offered release from the heavy days and nights of waiting. My imagination revisited our California years, when Betsy and I cherished our Mondays with our four young children along the seashore at Laguna Beach. We made sand castles, skimmed rocks, gathered shells, and scampered behind fleeting sand crabs among the rocks. Intent artists sat engrossed with their easels, capturing the essence of crashing waves and mauve sunsets.

On my return from the washroom, I stopped in the main waiting room to check in with the aging father of an adult son who was on the verge of dying from a horrific machine-shop wound. He could speak no English, but my daughter Rachel, who spoke fluent Spanish, established a gentle relationship between us. Week after week he remained there, sleeping on the floor in the corner or slouched in a lounge chair all night. Rachel realized he understood nothing the doctors told him, so, at his request, she interpreted the doctor's prognosis to him. He was immeasurably grateful to understand what was happening with his son. Human touch, a knowing smile, and eyes genuinely contacting soul to soul proved to be tremendous medicine for all of us family caregivers who maintained our respective rituals of waiting.

Rachel entered the waiting room, tapped me on the shoulder, and simply said, "Dad. Come now."

There was no code blue signal. I had requested the desk to turn off any emergency alarms for Betsy. Rachel took my hand and we hurried back. It was 5:19 P.M., already dark outside.

Approaching Betsy's room, I could see our family and friends now standing outside in the hall; everyone eerily quiet. I walked into the inevitable and unavoidable. The medical staff moved efficiently about Betsy's room. The ventilator, unhooked and relocated, no longer inserted oxygen into her fragile lungs.

Time altered as my feet walked me of their own volition to my accustomed place beside Betsy's hospital bed. My boggled mind split for a second, replaying for me the myriad fantasies: the many ways I had imagined, expected, and denied this moment. I looked down into Betsy's eyes. Her gaze returned unresponsive; lifeless. My hands reached as if they had always known what to do: placing fingertips to her soft eyelids, gently closing her eyes for the last time.

I closed my own eyes as my soul cried out to hers: *O Regal Lady, you decided it was time to go. On your mother's birthday, no less. Bringing your Soul Self as a present to your beloved mother, Ida Helen Garriott—to your father William, too, who may now embrace you free of the earthly judgment that ravaged your bond.*

How long did I stand there?

Rachel touched my arm, bringing me back into time, returning my conscious attention to the hospital room.

My mind shouted, *Betsy!* as a wave of searing pain burned through me. Betsy, my beloved, now shrouded in private quietness. Her soul slipped through the veil.

The doctor asked quietly, "Mr. Edwards, would you mind stepping out into the hall?"

I took Betsy's swollen hand in mine. "No, I prefer to remain here with her, if you don't mind."

"Of course. Stay if you wish," the nurse responded warmly. They gently removed the tubes and wires, the umbilical cords of death, which had monitored her progress and decline since the first of November.

When the medical staff finished their ritual of detachment, the nurse invited everyone back in. "Take your time. You have until 9:00 P.M. if you wish."

Slowly, family and friends joined me, each one taking a place around her bed, encircling Betsy in demonstrable oneness. For the next three hours, we took turns speaking from our hearts; goodbyes, reflections, poems, scriptures, special memories, and thanksgivings. "Betsy, thank you for . . . Betsy, I shall never forget . . . I shall always remember the time you . . . We send you Home with lots of love, Betsy. . . ."

Meanwhile, outside the hospital windows, a threatening snowstorm urged us to head out for our respective homes. Just before 9:00 P.M., one of the staff doctors entered and in a very quiet voice asked me for legal permission to perform an autopsy.

A millisecond of hot anger flashed through my body, imagining anybody poking into her body again. Enough of this! I understood how important gathered data is to medical research, but not this time. *Not on my Betsy. No more! Please, let her be.*

I declined, "You know, I think not. She has been through enough."

Everyone exited the room, leaving Betsy and me alone together for our last time. I sat down. I sat in the same chair I had been sitting in for a month. The chair had become my fantasy bubble, my meditation space, and my home base. From the chair I had leaned over the bed's railing, gently touching Betsy's comatose body for countless hours. Now as I sat, I noticed a vivid, pulsating, empty silence slowly cascading through my body. As I looked at her face, my eyes settled on her forehead and saw, as always, an ever-errant strand of curly hair. I stood up, reached over one last time, and gently swept the stray hair back into place.

I covered Betsy's expressionless body with a blue comfort blanket, embroidered with loving words from her devoted sister Lois. I pinned a printout of her favorite prayer, "Prayer of Abandonment,"[1] onto the blanket.

Fifty years of daily soulful sharing: in the twinkling of an eye, flung out beyond some unknown galaxy.

The urgency of the storm, the kaleidoscope of several gentle voices waiting for me in the hall, exhaustion: all these joined together; else I am not quite sure how I could have left her.

I leaned forward, kissed her cool forehead, and walked into the hallway. Just outside the closed door, a cardiologist nurse pulled me aside, "Mr. Edwards, may I speak with you briefly?"

I nodded.

"In all my twenty-five years here," she said, "I have never seen anything like your family and friends. I can tell that Betsy was indeed a very remarkable person. Your family is the talk of our ward."

"Yes, she truly is a very remarkable woman." I heard myself choose to use the present tense rather than the past. I

---

1  Fr. Charles de Foucauld, "Prayer of Abandonment": "Father, I abandon myself into your hands. Do with me what you will. Whatever you may do, I thank you. I am ready for all, I accept all. Let only your will be done in me, and in all your creatures—I wish no more than this, O Lord. Into your hands I commend my soul: I offer it to you with all the love of my heart, for I love you, Lord, and so need to give myself, to surrender myself into your hands, without reserve, and with boundless confidence, for you are my Father."

let it be. Confusion and a great emptiness ushered me out of Northwestern Memorial Hospital.

*Elizabeth Katherine Garriott Edwards.* Tangible and mystical reverberations of her energy remained, even in dying, touching us at the heart of it all.

→ 2 ←

# First Night

I awakened at 3:20 A.M. to the scraping rumble of snow trucks on our street. Reaching my arm over to touch Betsy I suddenly remembered—*She's in the hospital, and I will be taking the train downtown later. . . .*

I caught myself. *No! She is not in the hospital. She's not anywhere!*

I felt cold. My throat was dry. I got up and grabbed my robe and warm bedroom slippers. I shuffled across the hardwood floor toward the kitchen. I selected a glass and pushed it into the water dispenser on our refrigerator. The mechanical hum made a palpable contrast with the hollow silence.

I felt strange—awake but not. As I drank the water, I noticed how aware I was. I could feel each cold swallow warming up halfway down my throat. Standing in the kitchen, I could see along the hallway to the living room window. Outside, the single streetlight revealed a foot of fresh snow. White Death enfolded our house.

Panic surged through my body. I was a five-year-old boy again, longing for my Mama Jolly to tuck me in. *Pull the blanket over my head! Make my upside-down world go away!*

I took a breath and let the feeling pass. I finished my water and walked to place the glass in the sink. From the kitchen window I could see out to our garden. Mounds of snow blanketed our raised vegetable beds. They were shaped like graves, and I fantasized Betsy buried underneath. I wanted to walk out into the snow to join her. I longed to be tucked in beside her. My life force emptied into an endless purgatory of white darkness.

Then a memory arose, as if to pull me up from the numbing snow banks. Betsy was born in a Kentucky blizzard! On Christmas Day, no less: 1935. The snow was so deep the country doctor spent the night because he could not drive back home. Just six hours previously, all of us were walking to the hospital parking lot, wondering if we could drive home safely through the looming snowstorm. We all made it home safely. *Betsy, too.*

Suddenly, I could hear her voice, her warm alto tones softened with the faint cotton of her Kentucky kin, telling the magical story of her birth on Christmas morning to our children: "Mother told me that Father stuck a stick of peppermint candy in my mouth on my first day."

Peppermint! Our children did not forget Betsy's peppermint story. At the hospital, shortly after her soul left her body, Sam and Joanna ran across the street to a candy store and bought a bag of small peppermint canes. Standing around Betsy's hospital bed, we each put a peppermint in our mouth, and we placed one in hers. Peppermint coming in and going out. The taste of peppermint came vividly to my tongue.

The tension released. With a deep breath, I remembered it was the middle of the night and aimed myself back to bed.

Entering the door of our bedroom, I was assaulted by her absence. Rather than give in to the pain, I turned on my heel toward my office to retrieve a picture of Betsy. Already framed and sitting on my desk was the photograph of Betsy snuggling comfortably into her favorite dark-green La-Z-Boy. It was the last photo I took before the paramedics arrived that fateful day in October.

I placed the frame on her pillow and climbed back into bed. As I quieted, my ears grew attuned to the snow trucks outside, until silent exhaustion let me sleep.

## ⇢ 3 ⇠

# The Day After

Wide-awake without an alarm at 5:19 A.M. I was totally alert. It was twelve hours to the minute since she died. *Déjà vu, for sure.*

I turned and discovered her photo, exactly where I placed it. Her blue eyes blazing out at me. *So alive! Ocean blue eyes. Betsy, the lover of my life.* My soul spoke to her as if she were in bed with me, same as fifty years of mornings: *We paid our dues and earned our intimacy, didn't we, honey? Especially the last two decades of our fifty-year marriage. We made it through our midlife crisis, all four of our children grown and out of the house, with ten grandchildren. Like everyone, we have known in-depth; we had our share of tough and tender times.*

Our marriage could be summed up in Billy Hill's lyrics to "The Glory of Love": giving a little, taking a little, and letting one's own heart be broken. This was the story and wonderful quality of our love.

I drifted back several years into a writing workshop taught by Madeleine L'Engle, a very wise elder and author of *A Wrinkle in Time*. In a brief private conversation with her, I mentioned that Betsy and I were having a really rough time. Madeleine listened intently. Looking straight into my eyes, she said, "Hal,

13

my friend, every good marriage worth its salt goes through hell at some point, and if you two choose to grow through those hellish times, you will make it a much better marriage."

I shared Madeleine's timely wisdom with Betsy. We purchased Madeleine's marvelous book *Two-Part Invention: The Story of a Marriage*. How she and her husband, Hugh, worked on their relationship spoke deeply to us. We took the book with us on a road trip and read the book aloud the entire drive. Arriving home into our driveway, we were so glued to Madeleine and Hugh's story that we abandoned our packed car, closed the garage door, rushed upstairs to our bedroom, and completed the two final chapters sprawled across our bed.

Betsy and I loved each other dearly and wanted our relationship to heal and mature. We took courage from our love and consciously committed to enrich our relationship at a deeper level, to take good care of ourselves and to respect and understand our differences.

As counselors, we worked together with other couples. Most couples found ways to restore and enrich their relationships. We also worked with many who decided divorce was less destructive than a dysfunctional legal marriage. We gained so much from the couples who confided in us, vicariously learning many tremendous lessons that benefited our own relationship.

Returning from this unannounced flashback, I felt my body relaxing under the warm covers. I stretched my legs and arms, inhaling the tranquility permeating my empty bedroom. Voices from the kitchen alerted me to reality again. My brother Bill and my daughter Rachel were engaged in lively conversation over breakfast. Instantly, walking into the kitchen, the grief descended with a leaden weight. On purpose, I had to push through with self-talk: *Get going, Hal. You can do it. Stick your bread into the toaster and fill your coffee cup.* I greeted them, "Morning, dear people. Did you guys sleep well?"

At the coffee pot, I slowly inhaled the fresh brew. My eyes fell upon my unwashed glass in the sink and I remembered my pre-dawn awakening. I looked again at the raised gardens covered under mounds of snow, now gleaming in the daylight.

I sat with Rachel and Bill. The day's planning began. I would write and submit an obituary. Rachel would begin the calls regarding the memorial service. Bill would clean up the kitchen and living room. I would check with Rago Brothers Funeral Homes in Chicago regarding cremation pick-up details.

*Cremation.* An emotional avalanche! Betsy's body is being cremated into ashes anytime now.

Memory rushed in again. I felt annoyed. These unpredictable memories felt like unbridled stallions suddenly loose from whatever fencing had held them in.

I was immediately transported to my mother's deathbed in 1998. In a hospice facility, three miles from my brother's home in Southern Pines, North Carolina, our eighty-four-year-old mother was well into her sixteenth day without food, water, or any intravenous nourishment. I had an instinct to hold her, so I leaned over the side of the bed to cradle her frail and fragile body in my arms. When I said the words, "Mother, I love you very much," she opened her feeble eyes, looked squarely into my eyes piercing deep into my soul, eased backward into my arms, and offered her final breath. I closed her eyes and kissed her on the forehead.

Soon after, the family joined me. Betsy and Jean, my sister-in-law, bathed mother's body and dressed her in her favorite light-blue nightgown and pink slippers. Brothers Bill and Kemp pushed her covered gurney down the hall toward the facility entrance and the waiting ambulance.

Bill and the owner of the local funeral home were longtime friends, so Bill and I were invited to participate in the cremation. Together, we gently positioned our dear mom into the crematorium. I pushed the switch. When we returned several hours later, we filled a simple urn with her ashes. What some might consider an unacceptable experience proved to be for Bill and me, mother's youngest and oldest sons, a sacramental, gentle, and sacred privilege.

My mind returned to the kitchen. I looked across the table at my brother's face. As I tuned back to Bill and Rachel talking, gratitude filled my chest and made my hands warm. *Bill was with me at Mother's death then, and he is with me today.*

Bill and Rachel laughed about something. My action brain swiftly resumed. "Oh," I stood up, talking out loud to myself, searching for my cell phone, "I must not forget. I need to call Dick. He volunteered to pick up Betsy's ashes."

At the same time, my phone rang. I hurried into my bedroom. "Hello. . . . Oh, Hi Cathy. . . . Thanks. Yes, that will be great; yes, we can get on Betsy's obit together here at 2:00 P.M. Super. Thanks for driving over to help me with that."

Cathy reminded me, "Remember? I owe you this one. I'm paying you back, you know."

"Oh yes, I do remember. Thanks. See you soon. Bye."

I hung up the phone and thought of Larry, Cathy's husband and my very close friend. Since our meeting in 1965, our two families had become lifetime friends. When Larry died on June 21, 1993, Cathy asked me to officiate at the funeral. Larry loved his work as executive director of the Olive Branch Mission, a facility for homeless men, located in downtown Chicago on West Madison Street near Harpo Studios, where Oprah produced her famous TV show. At the Olive Branch, hundreds of homeless men arrived with tattered clothes and tired faces in an unceasing flow, a parade of humanity whose fortunes had taken a bad turn.

Larry asked Chicago photographers Sharon Smith and Wally Wright to shoot candid pictures at the mission. While mixing with the guests who frequented the facility, it dawned on the photographers that studio portraits with soft, flattering light might be a better way to highlight each person's individuality. Several homeless people agreed to have their pictures taken. Larry arranged to have their portraits exhibited at the Chicago Historical Society. Betsy and I joined a large turnout of Chicago citizens from every imaginable socio-economic level at the joyous event, giving great dignity to those Olive Branch guests who proudly stood next to their exhibited portraits.

Officiating at Larry's memorial service, I scanned the overflowing congregation, inspired by the gathering. They were both very wealthy and very poor; they were African American, Asian, Latino, Caucasian—all crowded together in a kaleidoscope of Chicago's multicolored diversity. I recognized several familiar faces of those who attended the photo exhibition at the Chicago Historical Society. I thought, *Wow! This eclectic crowd feels like a preview of coming attractions in some future lifetime!*

Rachel's voice interrupted my reverie. I turned to see her standing by the bedroom door, "Everything okay, Dad?"

"Yes. Hang in there with me. I seem to be falling in and out of old memories. Like a time-machine run amok."

The afternoon arrived quickly. Cathy and I finished writing Betsy's obit for the *Chicago Tribune* before suppertime. The rest of the evening passed in the same warp of details, memories, and emotions. I was exhausted.

Day was done at last. I headed to my favorite chair, set to my writing once again, and poured out the experiences of the day.

Ready to fall asleep, I entered my bedroom and discovered I had not made my bed; had totally forgotten it all day. I always make my bed. In childhood, all four of us boys were taught to make our beds every day; it was as natural as putting our clothes on. Our father managed a movie theater, so we grew up on newsreels and war movies during and following the time of Hitler. U.S. soldiers in boot camp were required by their drill sergeants to make their beds to be so smooth and tight that a quarter would bounce off them. I figured as a youngster I'd better learn how to make my bed like that, just in case I was drafted into the army. That image helped secure a lifetime habit.

Grief was knocking me off my practical practices so persistently that even my bed was out of order.

I straightened my covers sufficiently: Would it help straighten me? I kissed Betsy's framed picture waiting for me on her empty pillow, and collapsed into the mystery of another night.

# 4

# Memorial Service

It was Sunday. My granddaughter Sara stood with Rachel and me in the bedroom, facing Betsy's dresser. With warm patience, they waited for me to open Betsy's drawers for the necessary culling. Feeling awkward, I confessed, "This is my first time doing this in all our years together."

"You've never been in Mom's dresser?!"

"No. She always took care of her own clothes."

Betsy and I respected each other's privacy, especially our private journals and personal storage spaces.

I slid open the first drawer. There were enough socks to cover our entire bed!

"Holy bananas," I exclaimed. "I never dreamed she kept so large a warehouse of socks!"

We settled onto the bed to gather up the pairs. Sorting out the sea of socks, amazed at how different we were, even when it came down to the way we maintained our sock inventory, I was transported again into yet another recollection.

In 1975, Morton Kelsey and his wife Barbara invited Betsy and me to dinner. Mid-meal, Barbara asked, "Would you like to learn about your personality types and how you two are different?" We immediately declared our interest and filled out the Myers–Briggs Type Indicator (MBTI) questionnaires.[2]

Barb meticulously graded our responses, using her well-worn measuring templates. From the results, she showed us how our respective personality types accounted for the distinctive ways we approached life as extravert and introvert, how we perceived the same experiences differently, how we came about making decisions differently, and how we organized our time and space in different ways. These insights gathered from the MBTI applied to our ordinary experiences and made practical sense to us.

Understanding and appreciating our preferred differences neutralized many of our judgmental projections of "right and wrong" and "good and bad." This practical framework became a tool to practice patience, praise, and respect for each other. Remarkably for me, it offered an astonishing awakening to the reality that my most cherished perceptions were not always the whole truth regarding anyone or anything!

Had I seen this sock drawer before understanding the MBTI, there might have been another tense discussion between Betsy and me.

Sitting together sorting out pairs of socks, Sara's and Rachel's laughter eased my sense of trespassing. Slowly, as the day went on, the process of vacating Betsy's personal

---

2 The Myers–Briggs Type Indicator (MBTI) is an internationally renowned introspective self-report questionnaire claiming to indicate psychological preferences in how people perceive the world around them and make decisions. Katharine Cook Briggs and her daughter, Isabel Briggs Myers, constructed the MBTI. See <myersbriggs.org> for more.

belongings became easier for me—memorable, even playful—
thanks to my daughter and granddaughter, who made it
happen so naturally, showing off their mom's and grandma's
clothes in stylish fashion.

Among Betsy's belongings we selected special items:
sweaters, necklaces, bracelets, amulets, rings, earrings, etc.,
We arranged them on a folding table covered with one of
Betsy's white linen tablecloths passed down from her mother.
We placed them on the table in the living room from which
family and friends could pick their favorite item to wear or
hold during the memorial service, and to keep if they wished.

My appreciation of MBTI differences remained top of
mind through the week, as family and friends worked together
to create Betsy's memorial service. It was as if, post-death, I
was seeing our differences with new eyes. ENFJ that I was,
I enjoyed working on my funeral service, updating it every
year or so. Betsy, an ENFP, never once initiated any desire to
discuss her funeral or spend any time making plans for her
service. We often joked about my J and her P.[3] "You'll already
be settled in your own coffin to make sure it's comfortable
and organized before you die," she jibed. I responded: "Yeah,
and you'll be hurrying back home minutes before they put
you under, attempting to retrieve final funeral instructions

---

3 "J and P" are distinctions in the MBTI personality-type orientation that
describe our preferences for the way we relate to the outside world. Individuals
with J preferences are decisive and quicker to make decisions; you go to a J-type
for decisions. The shadow side of a J-type is making decisions prematurely,
without adequate data. Types that have P preferences are focused on taking
in more information before a decision is made; you go to a P-type person for
understanding. The shadow side of a P-type is waiting too long and missing an
opportunity to progress.

you filed away 'somewhere' in one of those awesome piles on your office desk!"

Here I was now with my sleeves rolled up, arranging all the elements for her funeral service, sorting deep into Betsy's awesome piles!

On the day of the memorial service, Bill, Rachel, and I arrived at the church early. I placed the box of printed worship service bulletins in the narthex, and then I turned to enter the sanctuary. There, in front of me was the prearranged podium for the guestbook. I stopped short and blinked twice.

I'd completely forgotten to order the guestbook!

The joke was on me: Mr. Organized! I imagined Betsy laughing. It was our laughter that smoothed our edges. Especially when we could laugh at ourselves during crazy times and get over it, whatever *it* was.

I inhaled my inner Betsy and took my slip-up in stride: *Oh well, forget the formalities.* I sighed and laughed out loud. To anyone watching me, it would appear I was laughing to myself. I felt I was laughing with Betsy.

The sanctuary was filled by the time we entered from the family room. I sat in the second row. Behind me, all around me, the full sanctuary pulsed with living souls come to honor all that Betsy had meant to them. Humbled and exhausted, I wanted to disappear into my safe cocoon. I riveted my attention on the bulletin, reading the worship service I'd created and memorized. Slowly my awareness gently opened to the music, helping me center. I took a deep, slow breath, let go of everything, and ran my fingers over the printed words.

*We Celebrate*
*The remarkable life*
*and*
*Our blessed Memories*
*of*
*Elizabeth (Betsy) Edwards*
*December 25, 1935–November 30, 2006*
*Memorial Service*
*Thursday, December 7, 2006*
*2:00 pm*
*Trinity United Methodist Church, Wilmette, IL*

The music soothed my raw nerves. Family and friends played organ, guitar, and sang the Shaker tune "Simple Gifts"; "By My Side," from Godspell; followed by the gospel hymn "His Eye Is on the Sparrow"; and Betsy's favorite song, from the Iona spiritual community: "Take, O take me as I am. Summon out what I shall be. Set your seal upon my heart, and live in me."

Host pastor, Kirk, and his wife, Susan, both dear friends, made all of it very smooth and easy.

Betsy's soul friends conducted a ritual. They had named themselves the Crones—a gutsy small group of generative women who met monthly, had retreats annually, encouraged and supported one another through thick and thin, and engaged in many outreach projects.

Holding long colorful strings, each Crone named some of the tender threads woven by Betsy's life.

Our daughters and friends read Psalm 132, "Enter into the Silence," and the passage from Romans, Chapter 8, that states that nothing shall separate us from the love of Christ.

Together, all present read aloud Betsy's favorite "Prayer of Abandonment"—the same prayer I had pinned to her blanket at the hospital.

When it was my turn to speak, I rose and took to the pulpit. Preaching was deep in my bones, yet here I was in the unbelievable position of memorializing my own wife. I looked down at my notes, then up and out into the hundreds of faces of love, sitting expectantly before me:

I think back to May 29, 1957. On the morning of our wedding, Betsy played the organ for our college graduation. The wedding was to be in the chapel across campus at two o'clock that afternoon. We needed help with last-minute details and our friend Harry Nesmith happily volunteered to pack and park our car in front of the chapel.

After the ceremony, we ducked through the tunnel of well-wishers from the chapel to the street, jumped in the car, and drove south to our Florida honeymoon. Our long conversations clarified our dreams. We both wanted four children. We shared a hope that having children would become one way we could enrich our world. We decided we were in the business of creating new memories, values, new traditions, for ourselves and for our family to come.

We found a modest motel near Nashville, enjoyed a southern fried chicken dinner, and checked into our room. Betsy asked me to get her suitcase from the car. I opened the trunk, the back seat, and back again. Where was Betsy's luggage? Harry had packed all Betsy's honeymoon clothes in the wrong car! He put Betsy's stuff in my dad's car, well on its way to North Carolina! In our car? Harry had packed Betsy's old textbooks, desk lamps, and everything you would never want during your honeymoon. I never learned if Harry did this deliberately. What a perfect metaphor for the unconscious baggage we brought into our relationship—only to discover it later on!

Betsy and I learned a lot about unpacking and letting go of useless baggage we no longer needed in our relationship. We shared a half-century sorting through chaff and wheat; the alchemy of hard work. Forgiving one another and transforming love ultimately won us both over.

I am thankful for Betsy—for her life, for her touch, for her presence, for her influence upon my life and the lives of countless others.

I am thankful for her music, her gentle and wise depths, her simplicity:

her seemingly supernatural intuitive ability to sense what's going on,

her indomitable capacity to forgive everyone in her life who hurt her,

her awareness that honed her great gift of processing without pretense,

her intention to transcend everything that ever happened to her,

her incredible honesty, her love for children and grandchildren,

her inborn awareness and insight into the heart of things,

her unlimited capacity for hospitality,

her love of cloth and quilting,

her gentle way of healing touch,

her ocean-blue eyes,

her simple lifestyle,

her love of family, flowers, mountains, and the ocean.

I am thankful that we worked through, survived, and learned a lot from our times of tumult, stress, misunderstanding, hurt, and stubbornness.

Finally, I surrender Betsy, with all the love of my life, into the Heart of Divine Presence and Eternal Love.

A wild secret thought momentarily interrupted from the back of my mind: *Do I? Do I surrender Betsy? Is this the end?*

I disciplined my focus and invited everyone into a few moments of silence together—soft as the snowstorm on the night of her death.

This collective silence was soothing, a palpable and healing balm.

Immediately after the benediction, I remained in my seat for a few moments, eyes closed, body and mind at the same time dazed and relieved. I felt a hand gently touching my right shoulder. I opened my eyes, stood up, and encountered a line of dear friends waiting to give healing hugs.

After the service, we gathered for a reception. We had arranged this time for folks to share a Betsy story. The grandchildren spoke from the depth of themselves in genuine expressions of love and appreciation. I could see Betsy's items worn among our children and grandchildren: her glasses, a sweater, a necklace; each item like a puzzle piece of her. People orbited about me, gently entered my field to comment on our children and grandchildren and their love for Betsy, for one another, and for me.

My friend Nelson sat down to the piano, filling the hall with ragtime and jazz. On the screen before us were a picture gallery and slideshow displaying Betsy in all her doings. Her face, the riveting ever-present smile, and her searing blue eyes looked out at us from every image.

As the images of Betsy washed over me, my mind called out to her: *Dear Woman, look at you! Aren't you something. You really are . . . were . . . are . . . a powerful, beautiful, loving, generous, soul-filled, spirit-led, vulnerable, and real woman. My God, my God, fifty years. Wow.*

More than five hundred people attended Betsy's memorial service. The depth of support and love that our family received that day cradled my broken, vulnerable heart.

We brought her ashes home and placed them on the fireplace mantel. Our eldest daughter, Lib, made four pottery urns: one to place in Betsy's flower garden in the backyard; one to place between her mother and father in Kentucky; one to take to Sunset Beach, North Carolina; and one to remain at home to mix with my ashes when it is my turn to die.

Back home and surrounded by family and friends, we were all exhausted, depleted, and glad to have one another. The glow and warmth from the living room fireplace was a wonderful contrast to the zero temperature outside.

The comings and goings of friends reminded me of the way people popped in anytime and sat around visiting in my childhood home. Barely a day went by when we did not have guests, relatives, neighbors, and friends in and out of the house. Our southern front porch with four rocking chairs, a ceiling swing, and a glider was the gathering place for countless friends and relatives. Betsy and I practiced this tradition throughout our marriage, providing an open circle of hospitality, supportive friendships, and a place to belong. Yes, being together as family on the evening of December 7 proved to be the natural way to conclude a very intense day.

Finally, I lay my head on my pillow. Shifting from being so visible and vulnerable at the memorial service to being alone was extreme to say the least. Although I needed it and welcomed the transition, I did not know what to expect.

Filled with bittersweet exhaustion, I reached for Betsy's portrait, took it into my hands, and gazed into her eyes.

*Oh, precious Betsy,* I thought. *What is happening to me? I'm enjoying these inner conversations immensely! I feel a fresh flow of communication with you that got lost during your final month of hospitalization and death.*

I turned in bed, placed her picture once again on her empty pillow, and continued talking to her with a full heart. I was experiencing no distance between us!

Betsy, you waited, so painfully conscious; you waited a long time for me to grow up. Tonight, I see so many things more clearly and objectively as a wiser old man. Is this increasing awareness a legacy from your death and grief's refining work in me? I'm just now feeling the impact of how you spoke up with sharp clarity so many years ago, and how the influence of your integrity still affects me. How often did you shout for both of us when I was too naïve and unconscious to "get it"? Now, after your physical passing, your courageous openness continues to imprint my heart and mind.

You were so brave and loving to confront my compulsions and infatuations. I unconsciously took you for granted. I was blind to the countless ways we males experience and exploit the feminine side of humanity. How many times was I a pain to your existence without even being aware of it? What will it be like if I finally see you on the Other Side, in a space where all is known, and nothing is hidden? I can only hope that a great Mercy will provide abundant self-knowledge and the grace to embrace all of myself. Oh

Betsy, I hope that God is as loving and compassionate towards me as you are . . . were . . . are!

I give myself to another night of sleep, grateful for you and the influence of your living presence even after death. Thank you and goodnight, dear woman, precious wife.

# 5

# Getting On with Life?

Everyone returned to their respective homes except my daughter Rachel and brother Bill. Family and friends spent energy and money taking time to travel to Chicago to honor Betsy with us. Genuinely indebted to everyone, I felt relieved to place the memorial service with all its intensity in the past and begin my attempted return toward "normal" living, though I knew very little about what normal living would be. With all familiarity of a normal life totally up for grabs, every circumstance seemed vulnerable to uncharted and instant change.

Bill drove us to Health Bridge Fitness Center. We exercised in the therapy pool, then concluded our workout by relaxing in the hot tub. The exercise was challenging. As I moved, my awareness came into my body and I felt a huge wave of emotion waiting to hit. I understood in that moment why many of my friends and clients neglect their self-care during periods of grief. At the same time, I realized how much more sane I felt, and that I could actually choose when and where to let the emotions come or not come. This moment in the pool was very reassuring to me. I knew I would continue my exercise regimen, and that I would benefit from taking care of my body.

When we returned to the house, I passed through the bedroom and noticed my journal still open on the bed from having recorded my dreams. I couldn't remember the dream I'd had that night, so I picked up my journal and read:

> Betsy and I are walking together inside a church. We come to what looks like a place to swim. Actually, it is a rather large baptismal font, and the other side of the font is a place to sit down and eat, with tables and chairs. I see a woman and walk over to her and ask her to go swimming with me. Of course, Betsy sees me feeling an attraction to this woman. I cannot help but see the concern on Betsy's face.

Hoo boy, this was a big dream. As was my habit of years, I brought the dream into my centering prayer practice. I relaxed into my familiar chair and let my mind float into the images in the dream. I explored each component in the dream as a distinct mirror revealing hidden parts of myself. As I paid attention to the symbols and images[4] in this dream, the following associations or insights popped up:

*Church*—my inner soul space

*Baptismal font*—my place of cleansing and new beginnings

*Betsy*—my beloved inner soul energy, my anima, or soul companion

4  Symbols, images, associations. These words will become more familiar to you as you explore how you can work with dreams and meditation in chapters 9, 12, and 13.

*Place to eat*—a nurturing space within my being
*Woman*—my sensuality; Aphrodite/Sophia, *kundalini*
(spiritual-sexual life force)
*Concern*—I am concerned about the reality of new
choices with consequences

As I reflected on that dream, I remembered waking up with libido. I had longing in my body. It felt strange to me, as it had been several months since I'd had any physical stirrings.

For fifty years Betsy and I experienced our fair share of ups and downs with *kundalini*, the life force of spirit and sexual energy. Throughout our midlife years we had known vacillating times of intense and gentle healing intimacy, as well as painful periods of separation; until the hard-earned rediscovery of an even greater intimacy evolved during the final decades of our marriage.

This time, taking first steps into an uncharted future without Betsy, facing my normal sexual transitions alone in old age, I encountered a waking-up experience.

I was glad I'd gone to the gym. I was also struck by the synchronicity of helping my body through the energy, even though I had not consciously remembered the dream.

This lifted moment was followed immediately by a flat emptiness. I had no idea what was next for me. I felt lost. How would I go on without Betsy as my daily sharing partner?

I felt a deep urge to ram these feelings down, push through, and get on with my life: *I'll work out, get busy, write a book. Something. Anything. Everything.* My thoughts, my will, my feelings were a kaleidoscope of unknowns.

Suddenly, a memory arrived full force, as if my agitation of feeling had made a phone call to the Universe. I remembered sitting in an office on the thirtieth floor overlooking downtown Chicago. It was the office of a dear friend of mine. He had just lost his wife of thirty-one years. I'd stayed side by side with him through this devastating loss. He'd asked me to write a poem to read while he placed his wife's ashes in their beloved backyard rose garden. A week after her burial we were meeting at our usual time.

I asked him how he was doing. He rubbed his face with his hands, then folded them together and placed them on his desk. With resolution in his voice he decided, right then and there, "Hal, it's time for me to get on with my life."

I remembered how his words struck me. He was a senior executive of a major corporation, responsible every day for hundreds of employees. This demanding position was going to provide skimpy time or space to seriously attend his loss.

That was that. He never referred to his grief again with me. He married again, retired in his mid-sixties, and died shortly thereafter.

I felt a kind of vertigo in the memory, as if I was actually looking out that thirtieth-floor window onto the fast flow of city life below. His voice repeated, like a waking dream: "Hal, it's time for me to get on with my life." One week and a few days after his wife died, he decided it was time to leave his grief behind him and return to the ongoing dependable familiarities of his work. He wanted to stay in touch with something still alive and functional. His life in the marketplace fueled his primary identity and life meaning.

But I was in a very different place in my life. I was seventy-one and retired from many years of commuting and struggling with how to keep a job, pay all the bills, help four children get educated and on their way, be a responsive father and husband, and retain my soul at the same time. Those were rewarding and challenging years. I'd failed at so many things; yet, there remained a solid trust that all my intentions and detours would somehow, by God's great mercy, teach me and hopefully point me homeward.

Now, I was without my parents, without teachers or professors, without a boss, and, after half a century, without my wife.

A seesaw of exhilaration and aloneness accentuated the stark and sudden realization. This was my time to summon forth my inner teacher, my inner parent, my inner boss, and my inner spouse. My inner voice had been guiding and awakening me, preparing me along the way. This would be my opportunity to embark on the next stage of my life.

The very thought of such radical transition evoked hope, courage—and anxiety.

I could not just *get on with it.* Perhaps, for me, there would be no such thing as returning to normal. Would this become my time to face my hidden daemons and unexplored opportunities as an old, single man, retired from full-time work and living alone? If so, I knew my stability required conscious and vigilant focus.

I sat up from these thoughts, reached over to the journal I kept close to my La-Z-Boy for just this kind of revelatory meditation. I wrote down seven deliberate choices:

1) Keep in close contact with my children and closest soul friends,

2) Call my regular clients and schedule them in, slowly get back into my regular counseling mode,

3) Keep current on paying the bills,

4) Continue attending my Thursday night centering prayer group,

5) Keep writing down every dream I recall,

6) Exercise regularly, eat healthy food, and

7) Maintain my daily meditation and journaling.

I would write it out. I would ask for help, for direction, for new meanings, and for signs to protect and guide me. I would no longer depend on others in the same way for my happiness. This was clearly going to be the deepest inside job of my life.

I understood that being alone and being lonely are two distinctly different realities. Grief was going to teach me, ever so slowly, how to live contentedly and alone with myself. Clearly, my happiness was my responsibility and my opportunity.

This inner shift was so powerful that my heart quickened with excitement, I spoke out loud to the listening room: "I choose not to waste away in loneliness; I choose to make something creative out of being alone!"

# 6

# Falling Upward

Then I got sick.

I'd been holding it together 24/7 for more than two months—attending Betsy during two hospital stays, commuting daily from the suburbs to downtown Chicago's Northwestern Memorial Hospital, navigating family and friends, and planning a funeral. An implosion was inevitable. I caught something: nasal stoppage, coughing, and a sore throat. Every nerve and bone in my body forced me to rest, to let go.

I took Tylenol for pain, Robitussin for my cough, vitamins, and supplements. Groggy and weary, I slept a lot. My sore throat and persistent coughing would not go away. Sipping on a cup of ginger tea, I fantasized myself like a piece of road kill. Then, with more perspective, I saw myself crawling through a reorienting tunnel. More hot tea with ginger, lemon, and honey.

My brother Bill fell sick, too. Angel Rachel fixed chicken-broth soup and mashed potatoes. After supper, I managed to join them in front of the fireplace. Staring into the dancing flames, I recalled the day I installed the new gas log unit. Betsy's asthma had become intolerant to burning firewood.

While she was in the hospital, I arranged to have a gas-burning unit installed. She never came home to enjoy it.

Grief-crushed again.

Weak and nauseated, I returned to my bedroom, climbed back into bed, and pulled the covers over me like a caterpillar cocooning. I heaved a sob then stopped myself—choking back the pain and stifling my sounds—embarrassed to be heard by my daughter . . . *and my brother. . . .*

Suddenly seventeen years old, I was wearing my number 43 fullback jersey, running downfield with the football held tightly under my arm. Duke University scouts were reportedly in the stands. I was the eldest of four boys in my family, the promise of glory. My father's dream of athletic success had turned to ashes when he injured his back while playing for Duke, followed by the Great Depression and returning home empty-handed to a $5-a-week job.

In my sickness, my tiredness, and my emotional rawness, this high school memory ran like a full-color movie in my mind: a waking dream memory. I was both in it and watching it. The felt sense in my body was a fierce force running to grab the win—and missing.

I had shattered my knee and lost the dream: my father's and my own. My mother spoke orders like a general: "You'll never play football again." I didn't. My two younger brothers did. They earned scholarships, took the field, claimed glory, and won. I was proud of them and ultimately released from the burden of carrying my father's unlived dreams.

Now, here I was in bed, curled up like a toddler, everything in me raging against this uncontrollable "sissy" emotion. Blubbering like a baby. My God, how old was this trauma? Seventy-one years old, fighting a seventeen-year-old wound?

*Let it go*, my inner voice whispered. *This is it.* The goal line I ran for was now the interior field of my own psychic potentials. *Let it go. Stop judging.* Emotion is not sissy; it's Sisyphean—it feels as useless as Sisyphus pushing the stubborn boulder up the mountain. To be a man is to *win*. How many men are broken, with souls amputated? How many have died unrealized because they could not stop listening to the shouting, cultural toxic masculine—an external voice made by fear and control—demanding a WIN.

I understood all this intellectually. I had sat in countless sessions as midwife and coach called forth and praised the courage of tears. This grief for Betsy was the most demanding emotion I had ever experienced. I moved my perspective and decided I needed to midwife and coach myself through it. With deep breaths, I quieted myself and attuned myself to my inner voice. In that welcoming silence, I could feel the truth of grief, the wider road and divine possibilities available to all who let go into honest, vulnerable hurt. To cry like a man. To grieve. To totally and bravely give myself to manly loss.

I wept. The limiting dam of judgments broke, and my truest tears poured forth until I was completely spent. Released. Emptied and quieted. I felt a peace beyond my understanding.

*For what profits a man if he gains the whole world but loses his own soul?* (Mark 8:36)

Many times I had preached that verse; now it came to encourage me. Awash in mystery and gratefulness, I turned onto my more comfortable left side and fell into the sweet release of trusting sleep.

The following night at the supper table, the grandchildren joined us. Looking at their beautiful faces, I burst open with more grieving. Though I felt an instantaneous urge to shut my tears down, I found I did not need to. My grandchildren, although surprised by Grandpa's crying, were totally accepting of me. I excused myself to my room, lay down on my bed, and let the tears have the time they demanded. Outside the room, I could hear the laughter of my grandchildren. Having them close by, doing what little children do, was a healing balm.

A tsunami of loss was releasing. Though it felt exposing, uncomfortable, and sometimes embarrassing, emotion was ultimately humbling me, allowing my vulnerable self to come fully forward.

Another day and another night of sickness. Coming through the worst of the cold, I was once again able to connect with Betsy's photo. This time, I took pen to my journal and wrote to Betsy.

What an incredible woman you are. Your eyes see my soul. I remember touching your cheeks and gently running my fingers through your hair as you lay unconscious in your hospital bed. Those final days still feel surreal, unreal, and at the same time downright insufferable. I feel your presence and your absence wrestling inside—like two opposing currents melding into one single movement. I sense your palpable spirit. Every memory of your penetrating blue eyes still pulls

me into the beauty and power of your presence. You
are my love, my precious love.

Sharp pain seared my broken heart.

I tossed and turned against the contractions of heartache.
Then I observed myself tossing and turning and made a
decision to quiet my mind. I let myself center in the familiar
meditating chamber built inside myself from my years of
centered prayer. From that perspective, I could observe the
grief like heavy sheets of rain, crashing and sweeping over
me, and then seconds later beaming sunlight cutting through.
These bouts of grief were a perfect paradox of unbelief and
gratitude: *Betsy is gone. Betsy is still here. How I love her! Betsy
is gone. Gone physically. I love you Betsy. Now here, now gone.
Both at once.* Then, unexpectedly, I heard the resounding words
"This too shall pass" in the low voice of a client from long ago.

Oh that powerful phrase, "This *too* shall pass"! My
memory took me back to Anaheim during the 1960s, when a
client named Jamie came to see me. She was the only African
American professor in the nearby community college.
Callous, chauvinistic insinuations from unconscious, racist
faculty members cut severely into her dedicated, courageous
spirit.

During one of our counseling sessions, Jamie shared her
frustration and hurt. Tears came and she reached for Kleenex.
After a moment of crying, Jamie lifted her head and her face
went still. I know the face. I'd witnessed it with clients, family,
and friends countless times. The face relaxes as the eyes turn
inward to a memory. Jamie paused for a long moment, then

took a deep breath and looked outward again, now into my eyes. Flushed with new energy, Jamie recounted the memory from her childhood. After being taunted by children at school, Jamie had rushed home in great pain to her grandpa. Seeing him, Jamie had launched herself into her grandpa's arms and received his healing embrace. A surge of enlightenment infused her entire countenance as she said, "You know what Grandpa told me? 'This too shall pass!' Tenderly holding me, he said, 'Jamie, precious child, this too shall pass.' He's right, Hal! Grandpa is right. This too shall pass!"

Jamie walked out of my office transformed by the vivid stimulus of her grandfather's spirit. Having previously died physically, Jamie's grandpa was totally present in that moment to his beloved granddaughter.

Gaining new strength from my Jamie flashback, I placed my journal next to my pillow, turned off the light, looked at Betsy in her photograph, and said, "Yes, Jamie. Yes, Betsy. Grief is now—and not forever. *This too shall pass.*"

Grief was not trying to snatch me or my manhood away. Grief was temporary, not a permanent state. Until this experience, I had reacted to grief as an agent of intrusion, something to resist, to get over, to deny and bypass—something to avoid at all costs. In truth, grief was filling me with more genuine masculine energy than I could have imagined.

Sleep came fast and deep. I awakened very early the following morning. A song floated inside my mind. I could hear my six-year-old grandchildren singing their favorite song, "What Makes the Sun Shine Bright?" They had decided to sing it especially for Grandpa during the Betsy Story Time following the memorial service. How precious is this gift of spontaneous and playful grandchildren! With a smile on my face, I went back to sleep.

Rachel knocked on my door at 9:30 A.M. "Dad: time to wake up," she said. "We're running behind for our massage appointments with Wes!"

While I was getting my massage, I cried again. Quieter tears, but tears again, poured from my eyes. Wes, our dedicated and gifted massage therapist, gently confirmed that muscles have memories. My entire body was mourning Betsy's absence.

When Wes discussed my upcoming massage schedule for 2007, he asked me if I wanted to take Betsy's usual noontime slot or my regular 1:30 P.M. time. Was I going to regress into a weeping old man? Here again, instant tears flooded my eyes with the sudden realization that Betsy and I would never take this trip together again!

Massage days were our time to share and just hang out together. Betsy would have her massage first while I meditated at the library or the chapel at the Billy Graham Center, just four blocks away. During my massage, Betsy sat in a comfortable chair in the waiting room, peacefully appreciating all the new releases in her twisted body. Having had scoliosis since the age of twelve, Betsy had lived with physical discomfort, shortness of breath, and limited energy during most of our marriage. Still, she gave so much of herself: she spent herself on me, on the children and grandchildren, and on the people who came to counsel with her in our home.

Wes was gentle with my emotion. We adjusted the schedule and Rachel drove us back home.

Grief made memories especially vivid. Sometimes it was hard to know whether I was in the past or the present. I decided it was best to nap while the time warps were on me. As I lay down, I spoke to Betsy, not to her picture, but *to her:*

I remember the very first moment we met. You walked through the entryway at the back entrance of Hughes Auditorium. September 1953, our freshman year at Asbury College. You wore those cute shoes— navy pumps with a narrow ribbon of rainbow colors. I looked up from your shoes and darned near tripped over myself catching my first glance into your eyes— your intensely soulful blue eyes. Our connection was immediate, a bit unnerving, even overwhelming. All I could say was, "Wow! Great shoes!" You laughed.

The sound of the mail truck brought me out of reverie into the present moment. I rose from my nap, meandered out to the mailbox, and pulled out the thick pile of official envelopes. BlueCross BlueShield financial statements from Good Shepherd and Northwestern Memorial hospitals, along with a letter notifying me that my health insurance had been *canceled* because I had not paid my monthly premium.

*Over a million dollars!* My heart raced. The amount of money was astronomical. *God help me!*

I dialed Tom Molder, my BlueCross agent. Tom assured me: "Don't worry about it. You have good coverage. You were under stress and forgot to pay your monthly premium this one time." It was frightening to look at the numbers.

Medicare and BlueCross BlueShield saved me from utter obliteration. Instantly, I imagined the hundreds of thousands of people doing their best to cope without insurance in similar situations. My mind quickened to the deplorable state of our national healthcare coverage; how our government has failed to act with wisdom and foresight.

Thoughts stirring from a heavy heart, I heard a gentle inner voice nudge me back to bed. I surrendered to it, climbed under the covers, and let myself sleep it off.

Weeks passed in this state of psychic bewilderment. Physical awkwardness accentuated my meandering pathway. I dropped things, tripped over nothing, inappropriately left doors unlocked or locked, turned left on Route 22 for no reason, opened the refrigerator wondering what I was looking for, and walked into rooms with no awareness of what for or why. I did not like my physical clumsiness at all. My friends encouraged me to consciously observe everything and to be gentle with myself. I listened and practiced, choosing over and over to accept this unpredictable awkwardness. I did my best to be present, to be aware of whatever happened each moment. I concentrated on welcoming the enormous resistance enclosing me. At times, I felt like I was playing some kind of weird game, a very important game, observing myself—observing grief become my trusted mentor, no longer some dangerous and destructive anomaly.

As I practiced this new perspective of grief, I noticed I grew more keenly attuned to my thoughts and feelings. I was more adept at noticing my inner world. My thoughts and feelings were further detaching from my sense of identity. I knew I was not my feelings; I also knew that all my feelings were temporary. As I acknowledged and observed passing fantasies, flashbacks, images, and fears that came to me unwittingly, I received new insights and deeper awareness. When I failed at this, when I reacted to circumstances personally, I caught myself more quickly. It was easier to step back and remind myself as I failed and fell, I was still falling toward the right direction: "falling upward," in the words of Fr. Richard Rohr.

Over and over again, the doors of my imagination opened without my will. Flashbacks and memories, like virtual reality, threw me back in time, most often into the thirty days in the hospital sitting in that chair leaning into Betsy's bed: vigilant to her coma, my hand searching for a safe place to touch her precious body intertwined within an octopus-like configuration of tubes and machines. The subtle bonding of her soul with mine transcended the ventilator and the concoction of high-powered meds, all of them having locked her conscious mind into an alternative state. Although she and I could not speak with our lips or hear with our ears, we remained spiritually connected, at a deeper level.

Yet "falling upward" did not always feel like falling *upward*. I felt myself falling over a high cliff, descending into a bottomless psychic abyss, spiraling and hovering in between that which was and is no more. I had lost what was familiar, tried and true. Would this emptiness I was experiencing ever be replaced with anything else?

The physical Betsy I knew and loved was absent before and after she died. I reached for her and could not find her. I called out to her and she did not answer. I spoke her name and a dark, empty silence replied. I could not believe she was absent. Every fiber in my being wailed out her name.

*How long, my God! How long will this last?*

Then, in uncanny synchronicity, while I was mired in disorientation and the temptation of hopelessness, I would receive unexpected and timely support. My brother-in-law, Ralph, emailed me during one of those heavy intersections, with the words of Kahlil Gibran: "When you are sorrowful look again in your heart, and you shall see that in truth you are weeping for that which has been your delight" (Gibran, p. 29).

Brother Bill returned to North Carolina and daughter Rachel left for San Antonio. My final drop-off trip to O'Hare airport behind me, I returned to live alone for the first time in a half-empty and newly decorated dream house. Opening the garage door with my handheld remote, I felt unexpectedly whisked into a life-changing solitude.

# 7

# Betsy, Present in Her Absence

One morning, a few months later, I had an epiphany that changed my experience of death.

It was a simple morning like most others. I sat at my kitchen table with my homemade mocha, egg over easy on a piece of toast, the *New York Times* and the *Chicago Tribune*, followed by my daily readings before going into my counseling room to sit in my meditation chair for centering prayer. I felt downright irritable. I noticed the mood but could not quite pin it down. I trusted my quiet time would show me what I needed to see.

I sat back in my chair, adjusted my legs into the half-lotus position, and quieted my mind. The dream I'd woken with asserted itself in my thoughts. It had been a big dream, so I was not surprised it wanted my attention. I wondered, Was it somehow connected to my irritable mood?

*The beautiful new sanctuary at Holy Spirit Convent is full; people are excited and waiting for the weekend conference to begin. I am finishing last-minute details, checking the microphones, and preparing to introduce the first speaker on the program. I notice a sudden hush across the room, and I sense that everyone is waiting expectantly, pausing for me to look up. I glance out into the crowd and I see this stunning woman dressed in a gorgeous sky-blue dress, walking down the center aisle toward me. I am astonished beyond belief. Betsy, now tall and straight, is smiling at me, beaming as she glides without effort, looking into my eyes. Everyone eagerly watches us. I look at her, and I weep with joy as I run into her arms. Everyone in the conference room claps and celebrates.*

I woke from this dream with a sense of awe. Betsy's lifetime of scoliosis—of physical frailty and imbalance—was over? Her jammed hips and ribs restored? The constant physical pain relieved? After a lifetime of concern for her physical suffering, I was graciously granted an image of her scoliosis and all the hidden hurts and treasures related to it fulfilled within the perfection of Greater Love.

I opened my eyes from this dream reverie in order to look down at my journal. I had entitled the dream, "Betsy Tall and Straight." When I lifted my eyes back up to return to meditating, my gaze fell onto Betsy's chair across from me. Betsy's empty chair.

Suddenly, I was riveted with an overpowering awareness of Betsy—a conviction that Betsy was *not absent*. Betsy was not *gone*. Betsy was still with me, vividly present and still mysteriously alive. In some inexplicable way, she was even *more* present than when she had been physically here.

This awareness of Betsy was so strong, so startling, I felt as If I could be knocked out of my chair.

I disciplined my focus so I could hold these two powerful realities in my consciousness. Betsy was tangibly and spiritually present even in her equally tangible physical absence.

My irritability had been caused by this tension of opposites just underneath the surface since waking from such a healing dream. Knowing the cause of the irritability released it and my mood immediately balanced.

Betsy's presence was undeniably genuine, even as I knew this realization was unfathomable, even weird from a rational or scientific context.

*Am I having a hallucination? Am I losing my mind? Is my grief playing dirty tricks on me? How authentic is this experience of vivid reconnection?*

For more than half a century I have maintained a regular practice of paying attention to my dreams, beginning in my thirties, with the assistance of Jungian dream analysts June Singer, Russell Becker, Morton Kelsey, John Sanford, and Helen Luke's community at Apple Farm. Over fifty years, hundreds of dreams provided first-hand timely warnings, insights, and encouragement.

I have also listened to thousands of dreams that brought clarification and healing to my clients. Time and time again, I observed the guidance, authentic depth, protection, insight, warnings, comfort, and healing given when individuals pay attention to their dreams.

I was also no stranger to intuitive insights and psychic phenomena, having experienced a life-transforming spiritual encounter as a teenager in 1952, and an NDE (near death experience) in 1987. I have researched the field of spiritual, psychic, and paranormal experience for decades, but this simultaneous awareness of Betsy's presence took me deeper into what I would call an experiential knowledge of the paranormal—human experiences that are beyond the scope of normal scientific understanding.

In the mid-seventies, my graduate professor at the University of Notre Dame, Dr. Morton Kelsey, introduced me to an abundance of solid research related to spiritual/psychic/mystical experiences. His semester course on "The Phenomena of Spiritual Experiences" provided a sound historical, scientific, theological, and psychological framework for natural numinous experiences. He taught me how to include and perceive beyond a rational STEM (space, time, energy, matter) box, opening me into a more inclusive worldview that included both the physical/rational realm and spiritual/psychic reality: dreams, ESP, mysticism, pre-cognitive data, déjà vu, synchronicity, intuitive telepathy, ancient and contemporary healing practices, NDEs, and other natural paranormal actualities. Dr. Kelsey demonstrated the obvious prevalence of such phenomena throughout our Judeo-Christian sacred scriptures, quantum physics, and mythology, as well as ancient and modern "coincidences" in all cultures throughout human history.

Kelsey's teachings provided extraordinary scientific and first-hand data embracing paranormal phenomena.

In August 2006, three months prior to Betsy's death, I had a precognitive warning of her coming death when we were attending the eight-day Centering Prayer Intensive at St. Benedict's Abbey in Snowmass, Colorado.

On the second day of our retreat, Betsy was too weak to walk back and forth to the meditation chapel. Her loss of energy was more intense than normal, and she struggled to breathe. Nick, our resident staff medical doctor, made arrangements for an examination at the hospital in Aspen. The doctors prescribed a portable oxygen tank and advised Betsy to remain in the Hermitage for the duration of the retreat. Her immediate response was classic Betsy: "My life is consistently busy and filled with people," she explained. "I really do relish this alone time. Hal, I want you to join the others for meditation in the chapel."

Betsy rested in the peace of the Hermitage while Nick and I checked in regularly and brought her meals. With Betsy comfortable, I remained in our circle of twenty-three people in the Meditation Center.

On the fourth day in meditation, without any warning, I was suddenly overwhelmed with sorrow. I saw myself walking into our newly purchased retirement home back in Illinois, alone—without Betsy.

I was reluctant to tell my morning vision to Betsy, but we had long ago agreed to share everything with each other. As I spoke about the vision to her, Betsy sat up on the edge of her bed listening intently, quietly attuned and serene.

"Betsy, I do not want you to go! I love you so much! I am so sorry for whatever I have done all these years to add to your pain!"

When she replied, Betsy's voice was strong, ringing with wisdom: "Hal Edwards, look into my eyes. Look straight into my eyes! Get this clear. You did nothing to cause this! You must never put that burden on yourself. Do you hear me?!"

I knew from my depths that she was telling a great truth. We both knew she was speaking to my lifelong self-created and self-sustained commentary that from my birth I was supposed to take care of others first, beginning with my mother, even at my own expense. The release I experienced with her words felt like a liberation.

On our final day at Snowmass, I walked along the pathway to St. Bridget's Hermitage at twilight. Fluffy clouds reflected a brilliant pink and deep purple afterglow. On a tree, silhouetted by the sunset, my eye caught sight of a magpie. The magpie lingered quietly on a limb, just a few feet over my head. I immediately fantasized that magpie to be our soul guardian and smiled to myself. As I continued my walk toward the Hermitage my pace quickened, so that by the time I reached our room I greeted Betsy briefly, grabbed my camera, and headed out again: "Honey, I'll be right back after I catch a magpie."

Magpie was still on her limb when I returned. She posed patiently while I clicked off several pictures, then bobbed her head as if to say, *Remember, you two are not alone. All of us here in the valley are aware of your pain.* Magpie launched from the tree and flew off into the night. *Yes. We are not alone.*

What a mystery!

My own life was a miracle of borrowed time. I remembered the time I ought to have died.

In May of 1989, I unintentionally severed a 7,000-volt cable of electricity while digging a posthole in my backyard. Using a three-foot-eight-inch gas-powered drill, I hit a major electric cable and shut down a mile-radius circuit of electricity throughout Northbrook, Illinois. At the moment I hit the cable, a cloud of smoke exploded out of the earth and I went into shock.

Within a millisecond I experienced leaving my body and ascending into a path of indescribably gentle light. While in that light I "saw" Trappist monk Fr. Thomas Merton lying dead and naked on the floor with live electric cords dancing across his wet body.[5]

"Waking" back into consciousness, I laid down the drill and walked into the house to pour myself a large glass of ice water. Everything felt slow and surreal. I drank my water and decided to go back outside to finish my drilling. The doorbell rang. Seven Consolidated Edison workers had swiftly descended upon my house. They conveyed to me the extent of the damage and went back to the yard.

I stood close by as a crewmember inspected the hole I was drilling. He brought up a piece of the inch-thick underground cable then turned to look straight at me: "Sir, you'd better get to the hospital. Your body is loaded with electricity." He paused, then continued: "You are lucky to be alive. We had two others like you this week. One is dead and the other is seriously hurt in the burn unit. I tell you, you are one lucky guy! Somebody was looking after you."

---

5  On December 10, 1968, Merton was in Bangkok, delivering a talk at an interfaith gathering. It was an extremely hot day. After taking his shower he stepped onto a live electrical cord and died instantly. This weird experience led me to Gethsemani Abbey where Merton lived and was buried. While attending that first retreat, six months later, Fr. Matthew Kelty, Merton's spiritual director at the time of his death, confirmed to me personally that what I reported in my vision was amazingly precise in every detail, according to what was told him.

Sobered, I went for an exam. After an initial checkup, I was told to go home and wait for a call. I was called back two hours later for a second examination. The doctor was shocked: "You are the talk of this clinic. Your initial prognosis showed dire results; however, your second report comes out surprisingly normal." Later, my cardiologist looked down at my gym shoes, "Were you wearing those when you drilled?" I was. "You would have become a pile of ashes if you had one single metal eye in your shoes." He seemed unable to take it all in.

Just as I was, at this moment, struggling to take it all in.

This awareness of Betsy's presence, this epiphany of consciousness, like that 7,000 volts of electricity, was real. I was not hallucinating. Grief was serving as a conduit, a catalyst to confirm that love and presence are not limited by time and space but transcend the boundaries of our normal habits of relating to reality. Betsy and my connection continued beyond our fifty years of physical union.

Ringing in my soul, I heard a line from our wedding poem; the closing lines of Elizabeth Barrett Browning's luminous *Sonnet 43*: "And, if God choose, I shall but love thee better after death."

## → 8 ←

# Hallowing Death and Life after Death

We've come a long way in facing dying and death and in preparing one another when the inevitability of dying and death comes our way. It wasn't until 1969 that Dr. Elisabeth Kübler-Ross, the Swiss-born psychiatrist who taught at the University of Chicago, published her now world-famous book, *On Death and Dying*. Dr. Kübler-Ross dared to bring the long-forbidden topic of death into public conversation, writing a dozen books related to the phenomenon of dying and death. She was a major pioneer in hospice care and helped transform the denial of dying and death into a sacred and viable service within the medical and social service professions. She wrote: "Death is simply a shedding of a physical body, no different than taking off a suit of clothes one no longer needs" (Kübler-Ross and Kessler, p. 82).

Betsy's death drew me to explore the natural inevitability of my own death and what it means to live my life fully and with passion into my final breath. This led me to read Sogyal

Rinpoche's profound *The Tibetan Book of Living and Dying.*[6] I was riveted to every page.

In the foreword to the book, H. H. the Dalai Lama invites the reader to focus on how all of us can choose to accept the inevitability of death, how we can be present to others in their dying process, and how we can relate to those who have died.

"Death," he wrote, "is a natural part of life, which we will all surely have to face sooner or later. To my mind, there are two ways we can deal with it while we are alive. We can either choose to ignore it or we can confront the prospect of our own death and, by thinking clearly about it, try to minimize the suffering that it can bring" (Rinpoche, p. ix).

His Holiness summons us to take certain precautions beforehand. "Naturally, most of us would like to die a peaceful death, but it is also clear that we cannot hope to die peacefully if our lives have been full of violence, or if our minds have mostly been agitated by emotions like anger, attachment or fear. If we wish to die well, we must learn how to live well; hoping for a peaceful death, we must cultivate peace in our mind and in our way of life" (Rinpoche, p. ix).

During Betsy's hospitalization, my first spiritual director, Don McClanen (to whom I'm indebted for introducing me to spiritual disciplines that enhanced my inner and outer journey), mailed me a pamphlet entitled, *On Hallowing One's Diminishment*, by the Quaker writer John Yungblut. On the METRA riding downtown to see Betsy at Northwestern Memorial Hospital, I opened the pamphlet and read the following words:

---

6   Some of the many other books I read are in the bibliography.

As one grows older and more devastating diminishments are undergone, if these deprivations, losses, and limitations can be hallowed, it is possible to become ever more sensitive to, and more perceptive of, meaningful coincidence. It is natural to struggle against diminishments, like Jacob wrestling with the angel. It is well to see that, in doing so, one is struggling against an angel and not to let go until one has received the distinctive blessing of that particular angel. Even if one goes away limping badly, the diminishment will have been hallowed by this blessing.

These words seared my soul and prepared me to take a more realistic look at the reality of our dire circumstances. The phrase "hallowing diminishments" stayed with me and gave me wise counsel as I came to that crucial fork on the road with Betsy, and as I continued to discover my own path.

Several months later, a day came when I felt an honest yearning to thank Betsy and say goodbye to what was. Arriving home from an errand, I parked my car in the garage, closed the garage door, and walked into the laundry room. In an instant, I decided this was the time to take a contemplative walk through every room in our house. This was my time to do it! First, the family room in the basement, then the garage, laundry room, kitchen, bedroom, guest rooms, and living room. Finally, I meandered into Betsy's sewing room, silent and obviously unattended. Never again would I peek in and see her passionately hovering over her nifty high-tech sewing machine, gloriously lost and found in the sheer wonder of making the grandchildren their own personalized quilts.

Purchasing her fancy computerized sewing machine proved to be a stroke of genius on my part. It was our very first withdrawal from our financial portfolio principal, and it served to enhance her creative appetite during those concluding years.

Betsy's final quilting project lay unfinished on the table, awaiting her return, without binding or stitching: a wall hanging of an ancient stone entrance opening onto an ageless corridor, leading deeper into an unexplored hallway enhanced by bright light cascading through openings along the way. I had a sense that Betsy would want it finished. (It now hangs, thanks to René Gorbold, who completed the binding and stitching, in my meditation and counseling room. A photo of the wall hanging, *Passage Home*, illustrates the cover of this book.)

I continued through the house, salvaging and saluting every memory of Betsy. I caressed her piano, now markedly silent. She no longer bustled about the kitchen. She no longer slept beside me in our bed. Her comfortable La-Z-Boy chair was empty. She no longer sat with me in our daily meditation. She was simply not there at all. Finishing my goodbye tour of the house, I reconnected with the emptiness I had felt at her deathbed: the sudden and complete absence of her radiant charm. Our empty house became her empty, swollen, limp body. Kneeling by the fireplace, I opened the flue and lit the gas pilot.

I switched off all the lights and sank into our favorite double gooseneck rocker. I gazed aimlessly into the quiet flames. Each gentle rocking back and forth soothed my spirit like a restful, wordless mantra.

The noiseless emptiness of Betsy's absence throughout the house transported me to the last time I walked through the home of my childhood and youth.

I was born in my parents' bedroom in 1934. Dr. Grady Dixon delivered me. Mama Jolly, my maternal grandmother, paid for that house with her monthly check from the government, which she received as compensation for the death of her husband, who was gassed in the final battle of World War I. Mama Jolly also made money cleaning houses and grading tobacco for the market in the aftermath of the Great Depression. She died years after we four boys had moved out, and Mother and Daddy sold the old homestead, relocating to a smaller house on the other side of town.

On my final visit to 416 South Lee Street, pen in hand, I sat alone in every room, reminiscing, and recording the memories that shaped the foundations of my life. Hours passed in the blinking of an eye, and I walked out and shut the door for the last time.

Rocking, reflecting without thinking, and staring into the peaceful flames dancing in the fireplace, I caught myself bi-locating again on memory lane, liberated for a few moments from sporadic episodes of heavy emptiness.

How long would this continue? How many more seemingly endless raw jabs would sneak around the corner and stab me? *Ever so slowly*, I felt little promises of relief and release. *Ever so slowly*, I balanced myself on my grief-and-relief teeter-totter. Ever so slowly, grief accomplished whatever grief does. Would I, without notice, be swept into yet another heap of grieving ashes? Oh yes, more than likely, swept under time and time again, and I would ride it out, again, and again—whatever it took.

Rocking quietly in front of the warm fire, I was now alone, in a home freshly prepared for happy times, family affairs, and the wonders of growing old together. It became clear that my work was to let go, to trust and graduate further into the mystery of unknowing. Instantly, I felt relaxed, sleepy, and more at home with myself. I stood up, stretched my arms, walked over and turned the fireplace gas off, closed the chimney flue, and prepared for bed and another unpredictable day.

Walking across my bridge over troubled waters with Betsy taught me to embrace and savor the present moment and, as they say in AA, to take one day at a time, sometimes one moment at a time. I learned how to take the next step facing a seemingly unending list of necessary chores. Formal legalities, policies, taxes, Social Security, family situations, unattended house and garden maintenance, monthly utility bills, and credit cards awaited my immediate attention.

A friend wisely encouraged me: "Hal, keep the balance between your outer and inner work; do one thing at a time; do not rush. During most of an ordinary life there will always be more potential and responsibilities to address. Do not closet or armor who you really are from your outside world, and do not allow yourself to burn out. Do not overwhelm yourself by focusing compulsively on the myriad of ever-present externals. Give your soul regular retreat times, spaces for rest and reflection, and simply do one thing at a time, the next thing." I took his wisdom with all seriousness and made room in my daily calendar accordingly.

In the squall of so much to do I often whistled or sang to myself the memorable theme song from the 1972 movie, *Brother Sun, Sister Moon*. Slowly and surely, moving *stone by stone*, I called and canceled Betsy's cell phone contract. Never again would I dial 431-1342.

Time took over and life alone at home gradually sculpted a more introverted and reflective Hal. It became a bit more natural over months and years to navigate my physical, social, and spiritual life without deferring or referring to whatever Betsy would choose, what Betsy would like, or what Betsy would surely dislike.

Surprisingly enough, a fresh new way of being in the world, my sense of finding and following what was mine to be and do, slowly evolved with minimal stress, claiming its natural rhythm. Initially, nonattaching[7] from my usual responses to Betsy's valued influence seemed awkward. I noticed an energy shift, a new psychic space, taking form. Gradually and finally, refreshing water and new vistas of hope emerged from my own inner well.

Grief paid my full fare for a one-way ticket to places I would never have chosen or dreamed possible.

I completed all the unfinished house projects on Betsy's list. Bathroom curtains—I remembered she wanted white curtains for our bathroom. I felt a little strange being alone at Kohl's choosing white curtains for the bathroom. I valued her expertise in selecting the appropriate fabric and style. Tears streamed down my face when I hung them and placed two new rugs on the tile floor. She was not there to enjoy it with me.

---

7  I deliberately choose the word *nonattach* rather than *detach* or *unattach* because I wanted to evolve out of those years, not forget nor dismiss them.

I sat in my rocking chair, gazing through the French doors of my study onto the backyard patio. An invisible pain edged up my throat. She never lived to see the patio I finished. I so enjoyed building it, knowing she would surely come home from the hospital and be surprised.

Weeks after the memorial service I had the following dream.

*I find myself on a mountain bike alone, going over huge boulders. I eventually come towards the edge and look down great heights into the sea. I am to climb down the edge of this abyss—what now looks quite impossible. I fear that I will have to let go and free-fall a great distance. I do not have a rope. I must decide if the risk is worth it. I know that going back would be a greater risk. I awaken not having made the decision about what I will do.*

This dream encouraged me to continue walking the not-yet-explored dangerous edge of my abyss and venture further into the great distance of my unknown future.

I noticed that my dreams focused not on Betsy's death but "around" it, more about where I was, not where Betsy may be.

The time came to venture into Betsy's unattended storage bins in the basement. This time I was alone, without Rachel and Sara. Relieved that I did not feel the initial heaviness and disorientation so prevalent during those initial ferocious months following her death, I began sorting through her things.

Pleasantly surprised, I felt more at ease, carried back into the memories attached to her belongings. My usual intention to spend *just a few minutes* almost always turned into short-lived hours. Sorting through her stuff obliterated any sense of time. That was when I learned that memories are laced with a multitude of buried feelings.

Sitting alone in the basement storage room, I set aside noteworthy items, letters, and photos in specific boxes designated for each of the children. I decided not to read Betsy's confidential personal journals—filling a large plastic bin, mostly written in shorthand—letting them forever rest in their hallowed confidential chambers. Before destroying them, I briefly considered hiring someone who knew Gregg shorthand to translate them. It took no time at all to forfeit that fleeting fantasy; I wisely honored Betsy's intention to keep her journals absolutely confidential. I have never regretted burning them to ashes.

When I called the credit card company and notified them of Betsy's death, deleting her name from our account, the phone receptionist expressed unaffected empathy for my loss, and that touched me deeply. What was this? Totally unexpected empathy, spontaneously expressed by an employee representing a credit card company? Wow! I felt moved by the gentle concern of a complete stranger, who, in one brief moment, ceased to be a stranger.

I took the scissors and ritually, ever so slowly, cut Betsy's credit card into countless pieces. Another outburst erupted; tears washed through and quickly tumbled into oblivion. That card represented a valid symbol of Betsy's freedom and, in our final years, our total trust in one other.

Almost daily, I found myself in spontaneous dialogue with Betsy. "Thank you for all the wisdom that's emerging from all this pain! Thank you for all that I am learning in your visible absence and in your mystical presence."

Something in my depths *knew* that whatever/wherever Betsy *is*, she is now more real and more present, and more supportive than I could even imagine. I had confidence that Betsy, as the photo of her wall hanging suggested, was perfectly liberated when she passed through death's open entrance into a new corridor filled with shafts of profuse light: she is forever her absolute true God-Self. I feel completely satisfied that I am now fully known and totally loved by her, totally forgiven and totally reunited into absolute Loving Oneness.

My grieving process helped me grow into the realization that the way I prepare for living is the same way I prepare for dying: by not grasping, but by surrendering into the Reality of Divine Love, which exists here and now and forever beyond my understanding.

In the same way each tiny drop of water returns to Mother Ocean, I imagined that all earthly creatures, born good and innocent from the womb of Oceanic Love, inescapably graduate beyond physicality into a more advanced participation within Divine Presence. Within this context of awareness, I came full circle, as it were, to contain and honor my grief and celebrate Betsy's presence made perfect in her absence.

Most of us will have absolutely no control over how or when we die. I have known individuals who entertained certain death fantasies, wishing to avoid the agony of endless suffering. Sometimes it seems like our very existence is too painful to bear, especially when depression and pain dominate one's life.

If I had my druthers, my ideal fantasy when my time comes is to die a natural death at home, in the bed I was conceived and born in, with just enough morphine or pain medications to maintain full consciousness and, hopefully, make me somewhat comfortable: no ventilators, my DNR legal papers signed and delivered, with no artificial means of keeping me alive. However, having dealt my cards in hand, I inevitably come to letting go of all expectations and wishes related to how and when and where I die. I inevitably prefer to trust whatever accompanies me into the Great Unknown.

When it's my turn to walk over the line between living and dying, I ask that I will muster the courage and serenity to experience what Cenacle Sister Irene Dugan, Betsy's spiritual director, said shortly before she died. Knowing medication would dull her senses to what was happening within and around her, she simply said to her hospice attendant, "No, please. I want to have the experience" (Dugan and Clendenen, p. 147).

Over several decades of attending the sick and dying I have regularly observed how we are tempted to automatically fortify our denial of death by spending more energy, time, and money investing in the slight possibility of extending our physical longevity, without focusing on maintaining a conscious quality of life. I hope for enough mindfulness, like Sr. Irene, to nurture my conscious experience of reality and to make choices that give meaning and purpose to those final chapters.

I suppose, at one time or another, we all have entertained fantasies related to our death. I smile to myself whenever I recall a news report about some wealthy elderly lady in California who chose to be buried sitting up straight in the front seat of her beloved pink Cadillac. Truth or fiction, it still brings a smile. It feels good to have a good laugh in the face of Death.

Those haunting, heavy thirty days of waiting beside Betsy's unconscious body taught me the importance of making proactive decisions that will hopefully impact my end-of-life preferences, and enable me to live and die in peace, sparing my family and companions unnecessary expense and anguish.[8] That, of course, remains to be seen.

My dear friend Nancy Hohfeler comes to mind. Going in for her usual annual physical she was totally surprised to learn she had a radical and rare terminal disease with no available treatment; she would live only a few weeks. Everything happened so fast. She met with her close friends and completed her preparations for hospice. She invited me to join her with her immediate family a few days before she died. Together, in a circle around her bed, I invited us all to share a favorite mental image, a snapshot, of Nancy. Nancy smiled. "I'd like to share first," she said, and she did. Each of her children followed suit, sharing sacred stories. That final visit I saw her doing precisely what I had seen her do for over four decades: share her story in a genuinely humble manner that continually encouraged others to open up to new depths of their untold stories.

Nancy, a generative and amiable octogenarian, died as she lived: a living reminder of gracious compassion. The Winnetka

---

8   Ten years after Betsy's death, I came across the *New York Times* bestseller *Being Mortal*, by Dr. Atul Gawande. This profoundly practical "bible," written by a wise medical doctor, is an excellent guide for anyone who chooses to explore sensible medical options for our natural diminishment, dying, and death.

Presbyterian Church was packed for her funeral. I asked everyone in the congregation to stand if they had ever been in a small faith group with Nancy. More than three-fourths of the congregation rose to their feet. We all laughed, because we knew the experience of being touched to the heart by her personal, open spirit. Because Nancy "lived well she died well," just as His Holiness the Dalai Lama said in his foreword to *The Tibetan Book of Living and Dying.*

Why are so many among us afraid to die? How many of us accept death as the greatest conclusion to a perfectly imperfect life fully lived? We are all going to experience our dying and death, just as surely as we all were born from our mother's womb. I think again of what Fr. Thomas Keating said as we discussed Betsy's death, with a sigh and a twinkle in his eyes: "Well, my dear brother, in the end it's all the same."

Sitting by Betsy's side in her dying taught me more than I ever dreamed possible. My gratitude grows without end.

I journaled this brief conversation I had with her one night:

Will you visit with me in a dream? Will you come and hold me some special night in the delicacy of our inner chambers? Will you take me by the hand and lead me through this confusing fog out into some passionate, flowering meadow? Will you sit with me by our glacial lake while glistening reflections of your inner light bounce across the water from your smiling eyes? Will you sit face to face with me and embrace me through the eyes and antics of our children and grandchildren as they "Betsy" me with their delicious

DNA? I am both comforted and haunted by your undying love on this side of our Silent Wall.

Reflecting upon St. Paul's statement, "For now we see through a glass darkly; but then face to face: now I know in part; but then shall I know even as also I am known" (I Corinthians 13:12), I believe that Betsy now realizes the entire legacy of her impact and influence upon others. From early childhood into her teens she suffered through primal abuse wounds, which she eventually transformed into one meaningfully fruitful life of compassion, leaving her legacy of wise caring and genuine presence. Betsy modeled for me a kindhearted way to live and serve others, and a conscious way to prepare for death.

The summer following her death our children and grandchildren gathered to celebrate Betsy at Sunset Beach, North Carolina. We formed a single line, then walked slowly with Betsy's ashes from our beach house to the shore. Standing at the edge of the lapping water, we each offered our final thank you and goodbyes, scattering handfuls of ashes into Betsy's beloved Atlantic Ocean. At that very moment, above us appeared an entire squadron of elegant pelicans. Perfectly timed, each bird tipped its wings directly over our final farewell ritual. Now that was one classy, mystical blessing!

## → 9 ←

# A Tribute to Grief

"To be close to people who are dying helps us die
and helps us live. Life and death are so close that
one supports the other."

**—Thomas Moore** (p. 267)

Let's make a toast, our glasses filled to the brim with a
superbly ecstatic wine. Let's salute the phenomenal mystery of
being born into human history, getting to Planet Earth in the
first place, and finally coming face to face with our inevitable
graduation. Let's applaud the legacy of every person living
and dead who has made a negative or positive difference in our
lives. And let's acknowledge our most faithful master teacher,
grief, who has accompanied us through many losses and gains
along the Way. After all, grief teaches us how to grow from
everything that comes our way. Grief teaches us how to let go
and take the next faithful step into ongoing Creation.

Most people ask how a person could hope to experience
the healing power of grief when every day our newspapers and
newscasters portray a perpetual entourage of agonizing images
caught in the aftershock of tragedy, heartbreak, catastrophic

damage, betrayal, injury, or death. Absolutely, life is clearly saturated and surrounded by death. How then could grief ever become our wise and trusted mentor?

Through sheer unawareness we have snubbed the incalculable good that grief delivers. Thank God, whatever the depth or cost of our loss, we can wisely, eventually, choose grief as a believably restorative companion. Grief, more than we could have imagined, faithfully remains our steady guide during our abandonment, exhaustion, heartache, stupidity, misery, trickery, betrayal, misfortune, loneliness, and suffering.

In the end, grief is ultimately about not clinging, about not holding on, about not manipulating the process. Mark Nepo says it so well: "Things that matter come and go. We can't stop life from flowing. All the clinging and holding on only makes things worse" (p. 336).

Thanks to grief aggravating my normal way of life, I now find myself saying I am one of the most grateful people I have ever met. Learning the value of nonattachment did not come easily or lightly. My grief around Betsy was monumental and, at the same time, seemingly unending. Slowly and ultimately, avoiding the temptation of taking short cuts, I chose grief as my trustworthy guide. Now, having experienced the wise mentorship of grief, I would never trade her gift of wisdom for anything I have ever experienced in my entire lifetime.

Grief's journey continues to encompass much more than Betsy's physical death and absence. Grief squeezed me into its complicated vortex and called forth a new awareness that assimilates and infuses grace into the best and worst of times. Grief encompassed those challenging years when we lost one another, when we failed one another, when we almost divorced. Grief encompassed my imperfect parenting memories, my relational and vocational mistakes. Grief's refining process eventually claimed a full sweep of my human history.

I am grateful to report, having more than a decade of experience under my belt, that grief has the magnificent capacity to bring a person full circle. Grief refines, awakens, and prepares us to learn from, and let go of, the old. Grief prepares us to receive a larger life deepened and enhanced because of a disguised grace always available in the ups and downs of our ordinary life experience. Grief has the audacious capacity to emancipate every foolish detour along the way.

When my wise friends suggested that I welcome and lean into my grief, at first there was knee-jerk resistance; my initial reaction wanted to push all discontent aside. I do not know precisely when or how it happened; somewhere along the way I woke up to the significance of grief's monumental gift— trust and loving nonattachment.

I mean, how unusual is this, how weird, how counter-cultural: to look grief in the face, welcome it as a healing ointment applied to an infected psychic loss, and "go with the flow"?

Actually, in many cases, physical death may not be a person's most stressful loss. Clients and friends remind me that the death of a marriage can evoke grief's darkest and sharpest wounds, especially in the absence of mutual forgiveness and respect. How common it is for one spouse to feel liberated while the other feels tricked or betrayed! The termination of a marriage often leaves a spouse feeling deceived, abandoned, and unprepared to assume overwhelming responsibilities. It takes a lot of courage to grieve the loss of a divorce and to take up one's life and move ahead.

I encourage post-divorced parents, particularly with young children dependent upon both Mom and Dad, to benefit from going together to wise grief counseling.

Whereas physical death may offer some degree of closure, loss through divorce involving children will summon a variety of challenges, choices, and consequences. Genuine love and sensible choices can help heal many of the hidden hurts lodged inside the hearts and minds of young children deprived of the security and community they need and deserve from birth. Usually, it takes intentional inner work to bring healing to those childhood hurts lodged in the adult psyche.

Whatever the loss—through death, divorce, catastrophic damage of a home, or a living death such as long-term terminal cancer or Alzheimer's—grief automatically and appropriately assumes its unique position to assist the survivor's mind and heart.

Grief initially comes as a whirlwind of bewilderment, a refiner's purifying fire, a balancing act, ultimately a potential saving factor. I do not believe grief ever comes to us to injure or diminish or punish. Grief's primary and decisive function, I believe, is to decrease our ego's self-absorbed hold on life and ground us into our deeper God Self.

Grieving presents life's most challenging paradox; it serves as a transformative passage between attachment and nonattachment. To become conscious of this fundamental paradox is to learn how to let go of the familiar past and trust grief's slowly evolving wisdom. It is a most courageous path, and, walking this path by faith, one can only hope that it will ultimately lead to purifying Love.

It is never too late to accept grief as one's master teacher. In the end, how we choose to remain consciously present to our grief journey may well prove to be a saving factor.

The choice is always ours at any place along the path, particularly during those unbearably disorienting hours when fewer and fewer choices seem possible.

I salute a dear woman, Jan Hudnut, who was dying of ALS. Toward the end of her life she could barely lift one hand. Bob, her attentive husband, attached a bungee cord so she could peck on her computer keyboard. Jan slowly typed with one finger: *I had more strength. Now less. Still have a choice with what's left.*

It is in our darkest abyss of unknowing that we will most likely come to trust that our grief process will not fail us. Whereas grief is about losing someone or something so very special to us, this huge descent into our personal chasm is at the same time preparing us for unexpected treasures we never knew existed, hidden treasures for sure, to be found in their own time and manner, inevitably evolving into wisdom, fullness, and gratitude.

We can trust and hope, and at the same time choose not to control, or demand, or expect. Observing the obsessive and narcissistic parts of our false self, always wanting to control, we shall do well to accept reality and choose to rely on our Higher Power. Simply letting go is not so simple to the ego. Grief, I believe because I have experienced it to be so, has the innate capacity to facilitate and complete a perfect work. It just makes good sense after all. We can all receive Ph.D.s for doing our good grief work, no matter how many mistakes we make going through our disorienting mazes.

Yes, yes, absolutely: our carefully designed personas will be shattered and refined. Grieving generates pure paradox; it will rip our false-self masks off, shatter traditional assumptions, outgrow former belief systems, and at the same time secretly safeguard our hearts and minds while it painfully and painstakingly transforms our lives. Good grief is a God-Work already operative within us, upsetting us only to set us up again for the Higher Good. To trust this wisdom path of grief is always our best bet. It's up to us. We keep learning that choice is ours, always ours.

The third spring after Betsy died, I was driving east on Route 176, heading to Home Depot. I wanted to pick up a couple pieces of lumber to finish off a backyard project. It was a beautiful sunny morning, warm enough for me to open the sunroof of my Pathfinder, a soft breeze brushing my face. I felt Betsy near me, sensed her presence in the breeze. I smiled. I felt comfortable and surprisingly settled in my relationship with grief. Here I was, three years along my grieving road, finding myself in a place of gentle acceptance, drinking in the beauty of the day.

*Car Talk*, my favorite Saturday morning radio show on National Public Radio, came on. As I passed the local Catholic cemetery on the outskirts of Wauconda, I *heard* this audible voice coming from under the left side of my front seat. The voice was so strong and vivid that I instantly looked down in that direction.

The Voice said, "Are you ready to have a life beyond grief?"

I was startled, but I remained steady at the wheel and kept driving. *Why . . . yes!* came up from my depths, and within that stark millisecond a great release swept through my entire being. I knew a primal shift had taken place at my core. Three years of heaviness disappeared like a fog surrendering to the morning sun.

I parked and entered Home Depot, wondering if the other shoppers could see the wonder in my grin. In the lumber department, I inhaled the intoxicating smell of fresh cut wood and thought of C. S. Lewis' astounding book *Surprised by Joy*. I was surprised by joy! The phrase repeated itself over and over. *Yes. I am. I am surprised by joy. I truly am a blessed man*, I thought, smiling to myself, as I paid for my lumber and pushed my cart out to the parking lot.

That moment of epiphany changed everything. A definite alteration of my energy and perspective shifted into place. From that day forward, whenever I thought of Betsy or bumped into any reminder of her, I felt a quiet and settled awareness of her living presence and companionship—and deep gratitude for it all. I feel that to this day.

*Behold, the old has passed away; all things have become new* (Isaiah 42:9).

"In the end it's all the same." Fr. Thomas Keating's off-the-cuff phrase echoes in my mind. In the end, through it all, including all the bends, bleedings, and bumps along the Way, grief faithfully heals from Love, through Love, into Love.

Looking through the lens of grief toward the afterlife, Fr. Thomas said: "I see [life after death] as infinite love, as if the whole atmosphere of heaven is filled with God as a kind of vibration going through us. I think that we are going to see and know each other in God, whatever that word means. It strikes me as a homecoming, us returning home to where we come from. All of our brothers and sisters are coming home as well. I certainly have a very deep hope that it is a transition into an incredible related life" (Keating and Boyle, pp. 147–8).

Loving through grief and grieving through love are twin partners on the same assignment.

In the end, grief and love become identical.

## *Part II*

# PRACTICE

From Tom and Consuelo Witt:

This beautiful 32x24-inch framed quilt hangs over the head of our bed. Following our wedding reception on March 23, 2003, Betsy took Consuelo's wedding bouquet and, using a technique called flower-pounding, pressed the flowers onto a fabric in a way that transferred the shape and pigment of the flowers to recreate the bouquet on the fabric. Betsy made the otherwise transient beauty of the bouquet to symbolize the permanence of the marriage we entered into that day. We will be forever grateful to Betsy for preserving the beauty of that evening in its many manifestations.

## → Introduction to Part II ←

# Practice

I know of no predictable, universal prescription for grieving that guarantees watertight results. Different methods, practices, and insights work for different people. What I did discover was how important it was to honor and respect how each of us learns from and grows through our shared grieving process.

How we go about grieving is vital to our health, our relationships, our spiritual growth, and our psychosomatic wellbeing. I encourage you early on to make up your mind to grow and learn all you can from your grief. Do not allow your grief to come and pass without exploring thoughtfully and freely. Initiate practicing any exercises or methods that will assist you in your search for meaning and purpose.

Grieving Betsy's death gave me a tremendous wake-up call to recognize and honor the inevitability and mellowing process of my own aging and impermanence, and to awaken the supreme importance of attending my life-giving, never-dying soul.

Working my way through this manuscript I noticed that I was using tools and benefiting from practices I already had in place in my life. These habits gave structure to my journey by helping me process and incorporate the shock and transitions that followed Betsy's last days and her death.

Therefore, I offer to you the five practices that formed the core of my grief journey: journaling, community-building, contemplative prayer, dreams, and an openness to paranormal experiences.

It is my hope that the following five chapters can help you take fresh inventory of your life experience and enhance your personal wellbeing, especially during times of loss.

## ⇥ 10 ⇤

# Grief and Journaling

"I haven't written for a few days, because I wanted first of all to think about my diary. It's an odd idea for someone like me to keep a diary; not only because I have never done so before, but because it seems to me that neither I—nor for that matter anyone else—will be interested in the unbosomings of a thirteen-year-old school girl. Still, what does that matter? I want to write, but more than that, I want to bring out all kinds of things that lie buried deep in my heart."

—**Anne Frank**, Saturday, June 20, 1942 (p. 2)

Most of what you are reading in this book came out of my daily journal. For over fifty years, I have kept pen and journal close by. Sometimes writing seemed nearly impossible. Sometimes insights, thoughts, and feelings flowed onto the page with incredible energy. I am also sadly aware that at times I left myself a legacy of unwritten and unattended pages that could have been incubated into deeper insight, confession, restitution, restoration, and new possibilities. Chalking that up as a loss, I still continue to find journaling a most forgiving and restorative companionship.

And there have been those priceless times journaling the words of my soul when I bathed myself in harmonious rhythm with everything around me. Natalie Goldberg's delightful quote, included in my introduction, deserves repeating in this context: "Life is so rich, if you can write down the real details of the way things were and are, you hardly need anything else."

Journaling, while I was mired in the depths of grief, took extra discipline, time, and energy. That being the case, having kept a journal for decades prior to Betsy's dying and death, I found it quite natural to express the ups and downs of my greatest loss inside my journal. Were it not for journaling, I might have experienced my grieving like a ship without a compass in the middle of an overwhelming storm. I am so grateful that I was introduced to this profound and simple discipline.[9]

*Journaling* and *journey* come from the same root French word *jour*, which means *day*. Every day, we simultaneously traverse two journeys, an inside psychic one and an outside physical one. Our inner world of reflection and outer world of action weave in and out of each other, like inhaling and exhaling. Sometimes they overlap; sometimes they conflict; sometimes they joyously flow together.

---

9  I was introduced to personal journaling by my first spiritual director, Don McClanen, in 1974, at Dayspring Retreat Farm, the contemplative arm of the Church of the Savior, located in Germantown, Maryland. In 1975, Morton Kelsey taught me how to do *active imagination* in journaling; he became my teacher and spiritual guide until his death in 2000. In June 1976 I attended Ira Progoff's Intensive Journal workshop. I am indebted to these three spiritual guides, who reinforced the importance of keeping a personal journal. Over the years, I integrated and customized these three sources to accommodate my own needs, style, and development.

Looking back over several decades of regular practice, I can say without hesitation that connecting my visible and invisible worlds through journaling helped me stay awake, invited discernment, and enhanced my stability.

Life takes us through temporary places we could never predict—conflicts, surprises, opportunities, disorientation: a kaleidoscope of opposites. Keeping an active journal develops a more informed perception of the whole of our life: our deepest longings, hopes, resistances, annoyances, and our grief. Gradually, as we write our soul words, we become more confident and less afraid.

Tapping into an inner knowing beyond rational understanding, journaling invites us to attend the gift of the Spirit within. We find ways to transform woundedness into wisdom, hurt into hospitality, and problems into possibilities.

Journaling stores and restores memory. Benefiting from the Chinese proverb, "The weakest ink is stronger than the strongest memory," we understand how fallible our powers of recollection are. When we write down experiences and insights before they fade into oblivion we naturally retain more detail and depth.

Revisiting a journal entry, whether it's a week or years later, I am always mindful of how I observe things differently. I'm frequently surprised to see how something that felt so painful, confusing, or disorienting at the time of my writing was transformed into another clear milestone along the way.

Journaling has endured as a traditional spiritual practice at the heart of the world religions for centuries, and I have benefited from the wisdom found in journals of so-called nonreligious writers. Whatever your religious belief, including if you're agnostic or an atheist, I urge you to venture into the spirit of your depths with pen, brush, or keyboard as you pay attention to the soulful truth that summons forth your creative spirit.

As you relate to life's ups and downs, your journal can contain all your life experiences. This practice is meant to integrate and transform all our experiences; good and bad, right and wrong, sick and well. Problems are normal and inevitable because problems are given to be outgrown and to strengthen our character, not to be ignored or solved. Everything that happens to us is an invitation to grow and learn. Recording the truth of ourselves keeps us honest and helps us benefit from all our experiences.

With just a few simple guidelines, those of you with little or no experience can immediately begin this practice without missing a step. You need not be a skilled writer to write in your journal. Spelling or grammar need never be perfect. The way you write from your heart is the way your journal reflects its deepest truth. Journal writing is more about intention than performance. Your best teacher is your regular practice. There are no wrong ways to journal. No one taught teenager Anne Frank how to journal.

Today is a good day to start. Give it a chance. Make a commitment to write at least a sentence or two every day in your journal for thirty days. See for yourself whether this is worth your time or not. After thirty days of journaling, take time to read through and reflect on what you have written. Refrain from judging your content or style. We are all in the mystery of becoming aware of what we already are: that we are all created by God's Love and we are all, each in our own way, seeking our way home, every day and forever, to God's Love. So, relax!

The recommendations listed here are simple, flexible, and reliably drawn from the tried and traditional experiences of many others. I offer these guidelines as a smorgasbord. Take only what seems natural and practical for you at this time. Let the rest go. Explore, experiment, and modify your regular practice. Let your openness and honestly reflect your life experiences and natural style. As your regular practice evolves, you will make adjustments that seem appropriate and timely.

Suggestions for journal writing:

1) Purchase a simple loose-leaf or bound composition book or, if your laptop or iPad is preferred, create your personal journal document with its own password to protect your privacy.

2) Write some of the significant events, experiences, questions, insights, dreams, fears, hopes, prayers, happenings, or images that seem noteworthy at the time.

3) Journaling can be an enormous lifeline, especially in times of deep grief, sickness, guilt, pain, or sleepless nights, or when you are overwhelmed, overworked, and too busy or too lazy to maintain regular times of contemplative quietness. Equally, journaling invites you to relish the highlights, and joyous, healing, and hopeful times. Of course, there will be times when journaling feels impossible or impractical. Even those

days are worth noting. For example: "I feel empty and stodgy and incapable of writing anything. I simply don't want to expend the energy to put my thoughts or feelings into words." (Then, wait quietly and patiently, and see what comes up. Write it down. You may be surprised.)

4) If journaling finds you caught in dark or hidden hurts, remain humble, and relax and surrender those images and feelings to your Higher Power. Allow yourself to be guided through these dark passages, and you will be guided! "Though I walk through the valley of the shadow of death, I will fear no evil, for You are with me" (Psalm 23). Journaling can be a soulful way to live into the question, to explore and integrate these dark periods. Journaling through darkness with trust in God lights up the night.

5) Seek to maintain a healthy balance between your inward activity of journaling and your vocational and social responsibilities, as well as your personal responsibilities. There is time for everything. Go for moderation and balance.

6) Seek out a dependable soul friend or a regular sharing group where safety, faithfulness, and confidentiality are mainstays, and, literally, a lifesaving advantage.

7) As you continue to maintain your journal, your imagination will become more enlivened. Practicing "active imagination"[10] will play a transforming role in

---

10 This method of working with dreams, developed by C. G. Jung, is further explained in chapter 13, "Grief and Dream Work."

journaling. For example, try drawing or painting, or writing a dialogue, letter, poem, or prayer focusing on the issues or images that deserve your attention.

8) There is no wrong way to write in your journal, so experiment freely and trust your own unique style. Don't worry about spelling, typos, or mistakes. Invite your whole self (just the way you are, here and now) to flow naturally onto the page. While you refer to and learn from the guidance and tradition of others who are further along, patiently treasure your own unique style, pace, and pattern.

9) Be ruthlessly honest and, at the same time, very gentle with yourself as you openly vent your feelings and expose your thoughts. Your journal serves as a great storage space and refinery for all kinds of feelings that would otherwise fester into a neurosis or addiction, causing harm to self and others if acted out stupidly. Anger, for example, is a gift to be expressed confidentially in the journal, never a way to act hurtfully to others.

The legacies derived from personal journaling have often bestowed gifts of hopeful direction for generations to come. *The Journal of John Woolman*, published in 1774, provides his spiritual insights involving the abolition of slavery. René Descartes recorded a dream in his journal where he wrote, "I think, therefore I am," guiding him out of personal chaos into clarity. Thomas Merton's personal and self-disclosing journals, especially his *Asian Journal*, forged global awareness of the importance of self-awareness, faith, and planetary interreligious connection. Henry David Thoreau's personal journals, written in the natural quiet of Walden Pond, enlightened Gandhi, Tolstoy, and Martin Luther King, Jr.

Dag Hammarskjöld, the Swedish Secretary-General of the United Nations, kept a personal journal, which was published after his death under the title *Markings*. The very personal pages in *Markings* reflected how the great medieval mystics Meister Eckhart and Jan van Ruysbroeck taught Hammarskjöld that "self-surrender" was the way to self-realization, and how "singleness of mind" and "inwardness" gave him strength to say yes to every demand and every fate life offered him.

Like life itself, journaling is an open book with blank pages inviting us to venture by faith into and through unknown and unlimited passages awaiting our highest good.

# Grief and Community

"A sense of community with all beings, human and nonhuman, alive and dead, gives us a true picture of what life is all about . . . you can't go it alone. To be your best self you need others being their best."

—**Thomas Moore** (pp. 239–40)

Back in the sixties, when Betsy and I lived in Southern California, our phone rang one night, just before midnight. "Hello. Is this the Rev. Edwards?" an unfamiliar voice asked.

I knew this person did not know me. Everyone in our church simply called me Hal. "Yes, how can I help you?" I responded and waited for more.

"Well, sir, I apologize for calling so late. I found your name in the Orange County phone directory just now. I know it sounds crazy, but your last name is the same as mine and that led me to contact you. You see, Reverend, my husband died several months ago and I think I jumped into the coffin with him. I can't get out. Can you help me?"

"Come on over. Betsy and I will put the coffee pot on. You be sure to drive carefully," I responded. Betsy called our good friend Mrs. Walker and explained the situation. Mrs. Walker responded: "I'll jump in my dress and be right over." She came in time to greet this total stranger with a knowing smile, saying, "I know something of how you feel; when my husband died, I wanted to jump in his coffin, just like you."

They immediately bonded, poured coffee, and sat together in the family room. A thankful and relieved young widow returned home two hours or so later, released from her agony because she experienced a personal touch, a wise and caring counselor, someone who had *been there*, and a new soul friend who would walk with her and provide ongoing professional and personal support. The wise saying in AA, "It takes one to know one," worked perfectly.

Every day during Betsy's hospitalization we were surrounded by a *community* of people sharing one common goal: Betsy's highest good. When it mattered most, I was sustained and surrounded by the loving support of other people.

Family and friends took turns sitting with Betsy 24/7, giving me regular times to rest. Betsy's sister Lois brought a soft blue blanket embroidered with a personal message of sisterly love, which I placed over Betsy's body at our final goodbye. Betsy's brother Bill took off work and flew to Chicago to sit close to his older sister during the night hours. Witnessing their tender caretaking, I was vividly aware of the unbreakable love these siblings had demonstrated to one another since childhood. Their mutually supportive relationships, their communications and their faith in one another, increased as Betsy's life diminished. In my heart of hearts I intuitively knew that Betsy, although comatose, was aware of being surrounded by loving individuals.

Neighbors stocked my refrigerator and freezer. The Fullerton Cenacle Sisters and friends living downtown housed our family members near Northwestern Memorial Hospital. A Palestinian ICU doctor at Northwestern quietly sat with me beside Betsy's bedside. A Muslim cabdriver found my cell phone in his back seat and ran through the crowded hospital lobby to my waiting elevator and stuck it into my hand. Dear friend Frank Griswold placed his arm around my shoulder as he held Betsy's limp hand and prayed for us both. Family and relatives traveled back and forth from Kentucky, North Carolina, Colorado, Michigan, Texas, and across the Midwest to offer love and support. Dozens of cards, phone calls, emails, and letters kept me afloat. Indeed, their heartfelt updates and personal stories nourished me. (I reprint some of these condolences in the epilogue.) I venture to say that none of these people realized the full impact these interactions had upon me.

Three words came to me as I reflected on the support system that surrounded Betsy and me: *community*, *communication*, and *communion*:

> *Community*—a group sharing common goals within a united reliance.
>
> *Communication*—sharing thoughts and feelings with one another.
>
> *Communion*—experiencing soulful unity in God together.

These three C's have well-established ancient roots that provide vital lifelines to human relationships, no matter one's culture, race, gender, religion, or political circumstance.

In normal everyday life, and especially during tough times, we are protected, guided, and restored through community, communication, and communion.

It took me a lifetime of experiences, including many crucial choices along the way, to discover and build community, to learn how to communicate and practice and cultivate an intimate relationship with God. I'm now an octogenarian and I'm still learning and growing, gleaning insight and changing.

Community is the thread that weaves meaning and purpose into the context of relationships. We were all born to explore and experience what it means to belong, to give and receive ourselves, and care for one another. I have struggled with loneliness and feelings of great darkness, emptiness, and abandonment. Like many of you, I have looked for love in wrong and stupid ways. I have learned equally through what I did wrong as much as what I did right in my personal relationships. I owe my mistakes and my successes equal gratitude. In fact, being open to others while being present to my deeper self enhanced mutual substance and trust.

Here are a few guidelines I have learned along the way:

1) Community includes two or more people who commit to a journey that acknowledges each person's uniqueness and appreciates each person's differences, always seeking the highest good for one's true self and for all others.

2) Community is about a dedication to mutual trust and mutual benefit.

3) Community is the slow and patient work of mutual respect, moderating different perspectives and values, creating an overlapping mandorla,[11] where far right and far left moderate into a "third middle,"[12] an even deeper wisdom of the heart.

4) Community-building takes effort, humility, and a commitment to grow and learn.

5) Community-building summons us to recognize and outgrow our resistance, to realize that *my truth is never the whole truth.*

6) Real community allows mutual vulnerability, a safe place for one's spirit.

7) Community places a priority on confidentiality, listening, and a commitment to win–win, not win–lose. "We are in this together" is our living refrain.

8) Building community focuses on the spirit of *Namaste*, which means *God in me welcomes God within you.*

9) Community positions us, in words attributed to Gandhi, to "become the change we wish to see" in others. This calls for genuine vulnerability and accountability on our part and genuine affirmation of, and openness to, others.

10) Community-building never diminishes an individual's true essence. However, the ego must, for the sake of the higher truth, give way to wisdom, welcoming

---

11 A mandorla is an oval-shaped "third circle" between two different circles partially overlapped. It energizes the creative tension containing both opposite circles, leading toward wholeness and balance.

12 This phrase, coined by Jung, signifies a space of union and transformation.

the deeper liberating truth of the individual and the group.

11) Community is an evolutionary phenomenon: never static, never to be taken for granted. Community may necessitate unlimited revisions to overcome seemingly impossible challenges and refinements.

12) The essence of creation, according to the Judeo-Christian religion, is based on community: "Let *us* create. . . ."13

13) Community is the necessary context for Love. If God is Love, God and all that is created by Love exists within Love or community. This law of community and love can never be broken; however, we break ourselves when we choose otherwise. The choice is always ours—to realize and to live in community— or to isolate ourselves into ego-bound illusions of separateness.

We all share deeply imprinted universal traits and experiences: especially during times of grief, when we are more vulnerable. When the light breaks through our cracked armor, our differences recede and we remember we are all, at our core, one humanity.

---

13 Elohim: The first definition for God recorded in the first chapter of Genesis is both plural and feminine in nature, energy, and gender, denoting God as "us" and "we." In the New Testament, the Trinity continues to stress the "we-ness" of the three-in-Oneness and the perfection of total giving and receiving at the center of creation and human community. All too often, we seek the results of community without being willing to go through the process of surrendering to the One Presence in whom we experience community.

## ✦ 12 ✦

# Grief and Contemplative Practice

> "God of the Silence: Calm and quiet my soul at the font of Your loving Presence. In Your silence, replenish me with a force for love, especially for those who are the most demanding. Where there is nowhere else to go, inspire me to drop into my heart and find Your life-giving grace there, weaving the fabric of human reality into a tapestry of love. Amen."
>
> —**Peter Traben Haas** (p. 239)

My first attempts at contemplative prayer made it obvious that I knew very little about how to simply stop and relax. I found it hard to reflect alone without reading something that slowed me down and pointed me toward my quiet center. My spiritual director introduced me to different ways to pray and think from my heart, with less cognitive work and more reflection. I was delighted to discover the book *The Cloud of Unknowing*, an anonymous fourteenth-century work of Christian mysticism, which is a spiritual guide for contemplative prayer. I was also pleased to learn the repetitive mantra called the "Jesus Prayer" ("Lord Jesus Christ, son of God, have mercy on me, a sinner"). This prayer is based on the Eastern Orthodox (Greek) prayer manual, *The Philokalia*, which was popularized by the nineteenth-century anonymous Russian spiritual classic, *The Way of a Pilgrim*. I practiced repeating the Jesus Prayer silently in my heart for more than ten years. I practiced hatha yoga at the Himalayan Institute and took their course on meditative breathing. I discovered how natural and simple breath-praying is.

In the mid-eighties, Fr. Keith Hosey and Sr. Maureen Mangen introduced me to the ancient practice of centering prayer, a very simple method of silent meditation that has existed since the earliest centuries of Christianity. They gave me a book, *Open Mind, Open Heart* by Fr. Thomas Keating, a Trappist monk. That book became my daily practical spiritual guide for more than a year.

I began by reading two or three pages each day before I set my watch alarm for ten minutes of practice; I was still too busy and insecure to actually meditate. Initially, I experienced lots of dark and ugly stuff coming up when I became quiet. So I reverted to busyness. I was unfamiliar with a method of prayer capable of flushing out unhealed residue from a long-forgotten past. Silence was not an easy option for me; however, my insatiable hunger for inner peace and intimacy with God encouraged me to "go along" with the program. I immersed myself in four simple guidelines, surprised at how simple it is to practice the Presence.

I attended conferences where Fr. Keating talked about how, at first, we may experience an unloading from our unconscious.[14] It was then that I awakened to my addiction to busyness. I grew to value and look forward to daily practice, ultimately sensing the need and desire to extend my meditation time to half an hour.

Black Elk's putatively war cry, "Today is a good day to die,"[15] spoke to me. The practice of centering prayer became my gentle way to *die daily*[16] as well as my opportunity to outgrow tired old wineskins[17] (perspectives, beliefs, habits, values, and practices) no longer able to contain the new wine bubbling up inside my spirit.

We were in our late fifties when Betsy and I decided to practice together. Our daily half-hour centering times became one of the most intimate experiences of our marriage. Throughout Betsy's dying and death, my practice of centering prayer remained as much a priority as eating and sleeping. My grieving process would have been vastly different without the grounding and sense of inner peace I found in centering prayer.

14 It is not unusual for beginners to experience "unloading of the unconscious" during meditation. During these moments, hidden hurts are flushed up into consciousness. It's like puss or infection drawn out of old, hidden, or forgotten wounds. This period of unloading may be quite uncomfortable, even though it is absolutely necessary, temporary, and transforming. This process is described in more detail in Keating's *Open Mind, Open Heart*.

15 Neihardt, John G., *Black Elk Speaks*: "It is good to have a reminder of death before us, for it helps us to understand the impermanence of life on this earth, and this understanding may aid us in preparing for our own death. He who is well prepared is he who knows that he is nothing compared with Wakan-Tanka, who is everything; then he knows that world which is real."

16 "I die daily" is a quote from St. Paul, describing his daily meditation practice, in I Corinthians 15:31.

17 "Old wineskins" (see Mark 2:22) are biblical symbols of old paradigms, outgrown traditions, and old habits and beliefs that no longer serve a person's ever-evolving consciousness.

Therefore, I encourage you to *be still and know* (see Psalm 46:10).

For me, the work of grief and the practice of meditation merged into one simple act: the gentle consent to let go into Love. I call it loving nonattachment. Grief proved to be a refining fire, redefining myself and my world through tremendous loss. You might say that letting go led me into the depth of Love. Meditation and the contemplative life became the conscious method for letting go and trusting God's presence and action within.

Grief threw me into unknowing. Meditation awakened me into Divine Presence, accumulating meaning and purpose from everything that came my way. Contemplation never took the grief away; it did show me the way through it. Contemplative practice showed me that surrendering into love is the transforming whirlwind in human relationships.

Centering prayer is a receptive method of silent prayer that prepares us to receive the gift of contemplative prayer in which we experience God's presence within: closer than breathing, closer than thinking. This method of prayer is both a relationship with God (our Higher Power) and a practical method to foster that relationship.[18]

As you establish a regular daily practice over several months, you will experience a sense of groundedness, a gentleness toward yourself and others. You will notice a growing capacity to turn resentment, hidden hurt, and hostility into hospitality. You will find yourself moving from self-centeredness to

18 This description of centering prayer and the Four Guidelines, and additional information, can be accessed at <contemplativeoutreach.org>.

compassion. There will be less anxiety and a growing sense of true self-acceptance, regardless of how others treat you.

You will experience a clearer view of reality and how to be present with less stress regarding your responsibilities. There will be a significant calm and deep trust as you take life as it comes to you. You will grow in your capacity to own your shadow side and let go of old hurtful habits.

In time, you will realize how miraculously loving and connected you already are to the entire cosmos. You will find yourself existing in a growing awareness of Divine Love fully operative within your being, regardless of circumstances.

Here are the Four Guidelines for a practice of centering prayer:

1) Choose your sacred word (such as Abba, Sunshine, Peace, Jesus, etc., or any one- or two-syllable word that honors your Higher Power) as the symbol of your intention to consent to God's presence and action within.

2) Sitting comfortably and with eyes closed, settle briefly into inhaling and exhaling and silently introduce the sacred word as the symbol of your consent to God's presence and action within, gently inhaling and exhaling into the Silence.

3) When you experience yourself engaging with your thoughts, bodily sensations, feelings, images, and/or reflections, return ever-so-gently to the sacred word.

4) At the end of the prayer period, remain in silence with eyes closed for a couple of minutes.

Years before I learned about centering prayer, I felt a deep gentle nudge whenever I read the small sign along a walkway inside the famous San Juan Capistrano Mission in Southern California: YOUR WORK IS YOUR PRAYER, AND YOUR PRAYER IS YOUR WORK.

Now, having practiced this quiet gentle way of Presence, I honor the profound and simple secret of that Franciscan axiom.

## ✦ 13 ✦

# Grief and Dream Work

"Without dreams, without the guidance of God through dreams, my life would have floundered and fallen apart. So, I am incredibly grateful to God for the dreams that have been given to me."

**—Dr. Morton T. Kelsey**[19]

When my mentor, Morton Kelsey, first met with his dream analyst in his late thirties he had no experience with dreams or how dreams work. He knew countless dreams were recorded in the scriptures, and he'd learned that every chapter of Robert Louis Stevenson's *Treasure Island* came from the author's dreams, but Kelsey had no personal knowledge or experience of dream work.

After meeting with his dream analyst, Max Zeller, Morton had a very brief and "meaningless" dream about a pink peach pit! He had no idea what such a dream meant. A man of exceedingly high intellect, Morton did his best to research what the dream meant; however, he returned to his next session utterly frustrated and confused.

19 This quote was taken from Dr. Morton Kelsey's unpublished papers, given to me personally.

Dr. Zeller asked, "What is the first thing you think of when I say the phrase, 'pink peach pit,' Morton?"

Morton responded, "Well, Georgia. Georgia peaches, of course."

Then Max asked Morton what the first thing was that came to his mind with the words, "Georgia peaches." Morton responded: "I'll be damned if I am going to tell you!"

Several sessions later Morton felt safe enough to share his instant association to *a pink peach pit*, something that happened in Georgia years before. This conscious association opened a blocked place in Kelsey, laying the necessary groundwork that healed a debilitating anxiety complex.

It is no accident that humans have dreams. Modern science and sleep labs tell us that our most vivid dreams come during REM time about every ninety minutes during sleep hours, from birth to death.

Dreams almost always speak through symbolic images, and we usually do not instantly and rationally understand the meaning of the dream. Yet, sometimes a dream will seem very clear. I recall awakening from a rare dream several years ago with these words: *Every moment is contained within any given moment.*

Dreams can reveal through imagery something we are not consciously aware of; frequently something we resist knowing about ourselves. You may recall at some time going to bed with a problem and waking up with insights on how to outgrow the problem.

Dreams come from a depth beyond the conscious understanding of one's rational mind. They are the royal road,[20] or the bridge, from our unconscious depths to our conscious mind. We will benefit from their wisdom by paying attention to them, beginning with writing them down.

An "aha" awakening often surfaces into consciousness when the dreamer returns to a dream after it has time to incubate or cool off. Journaling one's reflections on dreams often opens new insights and fresh possibilities.

For you who sense an inner call to pay attention to your dreams, whether you are in the grips of grief or simply living an ordinary day-to-day life, I assure you that paying attention to your dreams on a regular basis will sharpen your perception of reality and maximize your purpose, meaning, and highest potential. You may also choose to do your dream work with a spiritual guide. Dreams processed with a spiritual guide, analyst, or dream-sharing group can provide objective feedback and crucial direction.

I suggest the following guidelines as a simple way to work with dreams:

1) Place a journal and pen within easy reach. Ask your Dream Maker for a dream. Be patient, ready, and open.
2) Write down the dream just as you received it, to the best of your recall. Do not seek to understand the dream in any rational way. Snippets count. Write down partial dreams or pieces of a dream. Write

---

20 Sigmund Freud was the first to describe dreams as the "royal road" to the unconscious, a major rediscovery in the phenomenology of dream work in analytical psychology.

down whatever you remember. Don't fret over spelling and grammar.

3) Number, date, and title each dream entry. For example: Dream #45, 7/14/———, Notorious Jail Building.

4) Seek out a well-grounded companion who has a compassionate worldview, including openness to spiritual and psychic phenomena. Invite your companion to offer you his or her objective feedback to stimulate even deeper reflection.

5) Set your imagination free; ask the dream to open itself to you. Do not squelch the passion and truth in your dream with cultural prejudices or religious morals. Dream symbols transcend all rigid or literal moral legalisms of right or wrong. Let go and venture beyond your prejudices and resistances. Allow the dream to uncover the hidden, undiscovered parts of your deeper self, where transforming treasures of new awareness await you.

6) Every dream is ultimately for your highest good, even so-called nightmares. "Bad dreams" are warning signals coming to shake and wake us up, enlighten us, guide us, and reset us into a deeper truth.

7) Practice trusting your intuition by paying attention to the images, feelings, insights, and questions that appear in the dream or in your reflection of the dream.

8) Express your dream in a creative form: journal; write an unmailed letter, doodle, film or playscript; draw, paint, dance, adopt a yoga pose. Use any creative form that inspires you to deepen your relationship to the symbols

in the dream, and give honor to the dream through wise and loving action.

9) The ultimate gift of a dream is to reveal your own truth, to provide balance and grounding and call you into rediscovering your true identity. Dreams never manipulate, never shame, never diminish; they never shortcut or reject what eventually enhances your personal and social journey toward wholeness.

10) Dreams, I have learned through my own experience and listening to the stories of others, can guide us into our highest potential.

11) Working with one's dreams and practicing daily meditation can go hand in hand.

12) With the guidance of dreams a person can outgrow grief's tragic losses and life's greatest hurts, and harvest great fruit.

13) The more energy-packed the dream's emotion, the more your dream characters may project negative or positive energy upon another person, event, space, or thing. Ask the courageous question: *What is hidden within me that mirrors that highly charged dream symbol?* For example, you have a weird nightmarish dream about your stepmother and you wake up sweating and angry and ready to punch her in the nose. That is precisely the time to stop and ask yourself: *What is this wicked-stepmother-of-me saying about that hidden part of me that I definitely need to examine?* Choose in that moment to gather the courage, humility, and honesty to explore what your dark stepmother energy may

teach you about yourself and how you can best relate to both your inner and outer stepmother. (Whoever infers that doing dream work will be easy actually knows very little about dream work!)

Along with the association method briefly outlined above, you may choose to engage in the practice of *active imagination*, an excellent method of discovering the hidden meanings of a dream. *Active imagination* places you in the dream, so the characters, places, and events are given their own voice. This exercise has been practiced by wise philosophers, psychologists, and spiritual giants for centuries. St. Ignatius of Loyola utilized the practice of active imagination in his famous Spiritual Exercises, providing a first-hand experience of being inside the biblical scenes by becoming a character, place, or thing within the story.

For example, in the Parable of the Prodigal Son (Luke 15:11–32), you pretend to become one of the characters. You speak your truth through that image—imagining you are the committed father, or the wayward son, or the good, naïve kid who stayed home—allowing the drama to go where it will. Normally, active imagination takes a parabolic direction (i.e., the imagination journey usually descends before it ascends). This practice has proved its worth countless times. A beginner's booklist is included in the bibliography for those of you who wish to develop more expertise in practicing active imagination in your dream journal. An experienced companion, knowledgeable spiritual director, or trained dream analyst could lead you through this exercise.

This practice is often more "caught" through experience than "taught" by concept.

Remember, discounting one's dreams may also discount the presence and action of your Divine Dream Maker who knows all about you (more than you know yourself) and loves you enough to directly come to you and guide you in your dreams. I believe that is why St. Francis called sleep another way to pray.

We do not dream our dreams; dreams are not mere products of one's ego. Our dreams dream us, and the Dream Maker dreams us from the unconscious and mysterious depths of our soul, where the Presence and imprint of God eternally reside (see Luke 17:21).

## → 14 ←

# Grief and Paranormal Experiences

"Wherever I go and whatever I see in my heart and soul you'll always be with me."

—**Ken Wilber** (p. 411)

In her book, *Near Death in the ICU*, Dr. Laurin Bellg proposes that humans have not yet evolved sufficiently through scientific theory, language, or methodology to untangle our understanding of paranormal phenomena: "At present, we simply don't know. All we can do is observe the phenomena and try to understand them as best we can" (p. 58).

Dr. Bellg goes on to remind us that through cumulative observations we continue to search and outgrow the old hypotheses and make shifts in our evolving database that allow us to hold what we do not yet know in *curious regard*, rather than merely dismissing such phenomena as preposterous impossibilities. She encourages her fellow scientific medical professionals to regard mystery with reverence while we all continue exploring possible explanations until the question, "How is this even possible?" becomes clear.

Dr. Bellg understands why people are usually reluctant to share their mysterious experiences and dreams: "In our culture when marvelous and mysterious things happen that we cannot readily explain with our scientific theories and vocabulary, we are often afraid to share them for fear of professional ridicule, being labeled as a delusional malcontent, or worse, being accused of making up a sensational story for attention or some other self-centered motivation" (p. 58).

I am indebted to decades of experiences, study, and research related to paranormal phenomena and what it means to function in a practical way within a spiritual worldview. Naïve or doubtful of this larger worldview, I would have disregarded so many life-giving experiences that have proven to be genuinely effective signs along the Way.

Without an objective awareness of paranormal phenomena, such unique encounters with the spirit and psychic world would have passed by and disappeared like a dissipating fog, and I would not have recognized or benefited from their wise protection and guidance.

Since ancient times, our forefathers and foremothers have recorded numerous events describing a variety of spiritual encounters with the paranormal. For example, the Greeks had specific words for phenomena such as synchronicity, precognition, and reality beyond the physical world of five senses. They were aware of vital life energies facilitated through psychic awareness, revelation, love, sleep, visions, dreams, psychosomatic healing, voices, smells, ecstasy, trance, angels, demons, telepathy, premonition, soulfulness, meditation, déjà vu, symbolic thinking, etc. The Jewish and Christian scriptures, along with sacred lore from every major world religion, are filled with countless incidences encompassing paranormal phenomena.

Following one's intuitive hunches can be risky. My financial advisor honored my persistent concern prior to the drastic fall in the stock market several years ago. I acted upon an inner influence advising me to contact him and make immediate changes. He responded to my unusual request to go radically conservative. He revised my portfolio, saying I had the second most conservative portfolio among his clients. A few weeks later the average market fell around 46 percent. My loss proved to be minimal. To this day, I do not begin to understand the dynamics of that experience; of course, it certainly could have proved otherwise.

While going for a check-up on the status of my heart, I noticed that my cardiologist graduated from a medical school in New Delhi, India. I had been with other Indian doctors before; however, I felt led on this particular occasion to follow an intuitive hunch that kicked into action. "Doctor, did you by any chance have any connection with Mahatma Gandhi?" I asked.

His body jerked around. He paused for a moment, looking me straight in the eyes as if gazing through a window. "My father was Mahatma Gandhi's personal physician," he said, "and I would go with him as a little boy on some of his visits."

He seemed stunned and unable to continue speaking. I sometimes wonder what this brilliant surgeon thought about this total stranger asking such a personal question.

If I were to rationalize and dismiss the transformative mysteries of paranormal phenomena I would feel a sense of diminishment in my experience of life as meaningful. The recurring encounters of Betsy's presence seemed overwhelming and surreal at first, and over time equally genuine and natural. Today, her presence and her absence remain liberating and normal. I have become quite comfortable with this paradox. I have come to feel totally at home with her spiritual presence and equally at home with her physical absence, just as I have become more appreciative of being grounded in the visible world and actively mindful and attentive to the invisible realm.

This information is no surprise to those of you who have experienced lost loved ones visiting you, most likely in dreams, perhaps in a vision, or in other unlikely circumstances.

Chances are you did not share those powerful experiences lest you were perceived as some kind of demented idiot. All too often, people have genuine life-changing paranormal experiences that seem too odd and unacceptable. So, those potentially transformative encounters are closeted and left unattended for fear that significant others would dismiss them or even question their sanity.

Here are some guidelines to help you relate intelligently to paranormal experiences:

1) Open your mind and heart to the action and presence of a Life Force that exists as the Source of the entire universe, actively and intimately imprinted within the depths of your own psyche. This One Life Force is known under many names: Spirit, God, Christ, Krishna, the Dao, Chi, Adonai, Allah, Brahman,

Elohim, Jehovah, Ahura Mazda, Cao Dai, Bathala, Wakan Tanka, The All, etc.

2) Entrust yourself to a conscious relationship with synchronicity (which *Webster's* defines as "the simultaneous occurrence of events which appear significantly related but have no discernible causal connection"), including and beyond your five physical senses and your rational conscious understanding.

3) Take notice of the countless uncaused coincidences that constantly play a dynamic role in your ordinary daily life.

4) Commend yourself to this Higher Power that already contains you in a realm of mutual love, transcending and permeating your capacities to understand.

*Part III*

# GUIDE

From René Gorbold, Quilter:

Betsy and I were quilting companions. Encountering very curvy roads on my journey, I spent many months in personal retreats in Soul Catcher, the Edwards' backyard retreat house. The quilt, called *Calming Waters*, represents an unpredictable life of curvy roads transformed into a beautiful tapestry. "Love God with all your heart, soul and mind; and love others as you love your true self" (Matthew 22:36–40) became the guiding principle of this project. Hal bequeathed Betsy's supplies to me so several of her fabric swatches are incorporated into the quilt.

# Guide

Your grief experience is uniquely your own. I cannot say it enough: No one will grieve the same way you grieve. Value your own unique experience, your own process, your own stories. Do not bottle it up or "try" to leave your unattended grief behind you.

For some, it is easier to access the depths of grief than for others. Sometimes, it was easier to put my grief in my journal; at other times, I talked with a friend; sometimes, I needed to simply empty myself into the silence of my favorite chair, watch a ballgame or movie, or take a walk. Grief by its very nature, it seems to me, is a hard and demanding road to travel. Working intentionally with grief will in time bring about slow and beneficial healing, insight, and soul liberation.

I am especially hopeful that this book will be of help to macho-type men who find it nearly impossible to pay attention to their grief. Real men do grieve! I found that out. I learned that real grief delivered my manhood to me in ways I could never have imagined. Grief refines us into love and gratitude. That's what I experienced.

This inner work offers no shortcuts or quick fixes. It may prove to be a slow and sometimes demanding process.

Discovering meaning and new direction in the wake of a grief process is truly a worthwhile quest. Part III provides *quest-ions* to stimulate your quest.

In the words of Rainer Maria Rilke:

> Be patient toward all that is unsolved in your heart and try to love the *questions themselves*, like locked rooms and like books that are now written in a very foreign tongue. Do not now seek the answers, which cannot be given you because you would not be able to live them. And the point is, to live everything. Live the questions now. Perhaps you will then gradually, without noticing it, live along some distant day into the answer. (pp. 34–5)

Utilize Part III in any way you wish as you thoughtfully open the hidden treasures that will surely come as you "live into your questions."

# Questions for Reflection and Group Sharing

These questions are meant to be guides: tools for growing, awareness, and encouragement as you seek deeper meanings in relationship to your unique loss.

Are you ready to jump in and learn from your grief? You alone determine whether it's too early and raw, or whether you prefer to ignore it or put it off until later.

Perhaps you have an inner sense that this may be your time to jump in. You may feel you are ready to take first steps to unearth the treasures hidden inside your great sense of loss. You alone will know.

Here are four questions drawn from each of the first fourteen chapters. Select only those questions that seem to call out to you, and leave the rest until later.

It may help to jot down any key insights that come to mind as you reflect on any question. This simple exercise could hopefully open a few doors to your feelings, stimulate your imagination, and recall forgotten memories.

Let these questions serve as spotlights that focus on and value the uniqueness of your personal story. The purpose of these questions is to shake, stir, and awaken what is already known to you. Discern what is yours and what is not.

Take your time; go slowly. Think through these questions with your heart. Each question is designed help you own your story as you revisit the correlating chapters in my story. Stop whenever you wish; do not rush or take in too much. Honor your capacity and readiness to take in bite-sized amounts at a time. Grief slowly and faithfully guides us through the dark forest out into new passageways of creative beginnings.

Reflecting on my story through these questions you will inevitably respond, *No that is not what I experienced . . . no, that is not what happened to me*, and sometimes you may respond, *Yes, I know how that feels . . . yes, that also happened to me.* Pay attention to what you experienced, what actually happened to you, and write your own narrative. That is the purpose of the following.

## 1: A Surreal Moment in Real Time

1) Sit comfortably, take a few deep breaths, and relax. Ask yourself: *Is this my time to begin a practice of reflecting and journaling?* If your answer is *yes*, ask yourself: *What do I hope to gain from this practice?* Write your hopes in your journal. If the answer is *no*, what healthy choices come to you?

2) What are your most vivid or recurring memories and feelings associated with your moment of deepest loss? Describe briefly.

3) Using your active imagination, return to that time and place where you first realized that your life would

forever be different. Imagine a dependable friend sitting beside you and safely let go and open yourself to Love's healing Presence. Whatever comes to you, negative or positive, happy or sad, simply welcome it without evaluating it, and write it down in your journal.

4) Confronting your experience of loss, in the quiet of your heart, imagine being back in that moment of your heavy loss, and, when you are ready, say these words— the Welcoming Prayer of Mary Mrozowski—aloud: "Welcome, welcome, welcome. I welcome whatever comes to me in this moment. I know this is for my healing. I welcome all thoughts, feelings, emotions, and conditions. I let go of my desire for security. I let go of my desire for approval. I let go of my desire for control. I let go of my desire to change any situation, condition, person, or myself. I open now into the love and presence of God and the healing action and grace within."

## 2: First Night

1) Where did you spend your first night in the wake of your great loss, and with whom? Take two deep, gentle breaths; relax; and then identify and write down any memories of disorientation, fear, release, fantasy, guilt, or other reactions you recall having in the wake of your beloved's leaving.

2) What did you do? Where did you go? How did you seek ways to cope with your sudden grief? Sketch a simple picture in your journal, or a rough abstract

image that may reflect a memory evoked by these questions.

3) Identify and record in your journal any significant shifts or major changes that you had to make in your lifestyle, family, work, etc. Did your faith play a major role in the way you related to your loss? If so, how? If not, what did?

4) Sit quietly for three minutes with your hand over your heart, breathing gently, letting go. Invite any newly emerging feelings that may have been frozen, denied, or previously overlooked. Write those feelings in your journal that emerge as you go through this guided meditation. If you wish, choose a feeling and treat it like another person and write a letter to that particular feeling, and then have that personified feeling write you back. Go back and forth, recording the dialogue.

### 3: The Day After

1) Do you remember how you took care of yourself in the wake of your immediate loss? What would you have to let go of in order to carve out time/s for yourself in the midst of your very active lifestyle? Record in your journal specific ways you have learned to take care of yourself.

2) Are you ready (or would you like to become ready) to embrace any lingering or hidden hurts, or initiate genuine forgiveness and self-caring? Answer three questions in your journal: *What would it mean for me*

*to embrace my grief? What would it take for me to make
amends, to be ready to forgive* _____ (God, yourself, or
another person)*? Do I choose to learn how to embrace my
grief and grow through my loss?*

3) Sometimes a death or divorce, or any major loss, will
stir up other related losses, creating a domino effect.
Might that be part of your grief-healing process?
Respond to these questions in your journal: *What
lingering losses from my past am I aware of that creep
out of the shadows into my current loss? What seems
similar, or what seems very different in the overlap of
these losses?*

4) Go and sit in a restful and inviting place: close your
eyes, breathe into the quiet, and imagine being in a
field of Healing Light beyond everything hurtful and
healing, beyond everything right and wrong. Open
your heart into the Presence, invite peace into your
body, and surrender into the sacred silence. Inhale
loving kindness and exhale all resistance, then rest
without thinking. Briefly journal how you experience
this exercise.

## 4: Memorial Service

1) Sit still and allow your heart to rest quietly, as you
gently return in your imagination to the places
and times you participated in the funeral or events
surrounding the death and burial of your loved one.
(If there was no funeral and other circumstances that
defined this memory-event, choose any place in your

memory, journal in hand, and describe what it was like, and what you can do now.)

2) Record your most vivid memory during the funeral or memorial service.

3) Did you recall any special or mystical activities related to the funeral or memorial service? If so, list them in your journal. How did those encounters affect you?

4) Invite into your imagination a most trusted soul friend to come along and revisit the ceremony and cemetery. What else comes to you as you go back into that memory? Anything different, or new, or significant? Write it in your journal.

## 5: Getting On with Life

1) Journal in hand, take some deep quiet breaths, write down the name(s) of the person(s) who stepped up and supported you, if any, before/during/after your great loss. Did they play a vital role in your transition? If so, how was that for you?

2) Where did you go and what did you do that helped you ground yourself in everyday life? Tell your journal about any spiritual or relational support that made a difference in your life.

3) Imagine going ahead with life without your loved one. Imagine yourself holding out your arms welcoming the unknown, allowing yourself to trust without understanding. Write how that feels, at this juncture, in your journal.

4) List ten necessary things you need to do today. Then circle the two most important things on that list. Finally, underline the one simple next step that comes clearly to you. Inhale and exhale gently, get up and do what is yours to do in a heartfelt way.

## 6: Falling Upward

1) Go to your journal and briefly list the times you completely came unglued, when your grief and sense of loss disoriented and dissolved you with confusion, anger, rage, numbness, or psychic pain.

2) Identify and name both the positive and negative emotions that accompanied these times of "falling upward."

3) Did you ever come into a period of release, of letting go, of change?

4) If not, write your current hopes, fears, or doubts in your journal. Describe as best you can what you have learned so far from this descent into darkness. Finally, list the various options that come to you now—and write down the wisest choice that you now choose.

## 7: Betsy, Present in Her Absence

1) Can you recognize any new depths or insights that surfaced in the up-and-down fluctuations of your loss? If so, write them in your journal and quietly acknowledge them with respect.

2) Briefly note any unusual, mystical, spiritual, or para-normal experience(s) that happened to you during

your loss, including any dreams, premonitions, fantasies, or insights that came to you at that time.

3) How, if at all, has grief awakened you into a different perception of reality? Do you recognize any ways that grief shifted your self-awareness, your habits, your ways of experiencing yourself? If so, write it in your journal. If not, write your resistances, responses, or reactions to these questions.

4) Find a comfortable space near the light, journal in hand. Imagine sitting face to face with your beloved; imagine his/her spirit tuning into your spirit. Imagine what it is like knowing that souls do not die. Speak spirit to spirit to your loved one and write down what you say and what your loved one says back to you.

## 8: Hallowing Death and Life after Death

1) Have you ever had a close call with death, perhaps an NDE (near death experience)? What did it teach you about the inevitability of your own death and life beyond?

2) Journal in hand, sitting in an empty psychic space, ready to listen and receive, imagine interviewing grief and asking, *Well now, grief, what do you want to teach me? How can you take care of my brokenness, my great sense of loss and disorientation?* Write down what grief says back to you and continue the dialogue until it brings you home to yourself.

3) Sitting still, quiet and gentle, imagine facing your own inevitable diminishment, your own time of dying

and death. Imagine yourself at any age about to die. Name the feelings that come. Name the hopes and fears that come. List what you would want that time in your life to reveal to you. Write these thoughts and feelings in your journal. Write your own brief epitaph in your journal.

4) Journal in hand, pretend that you are physically dead, and your spirit is in transition between here and the hereafter. Imagine being totally surprised, totally known, and totally aware of everything. Imagine everything becoming absolutely clear: all your intentions, actions, thoughts, and influences created during your earthly tenure. Write down what comes to you.

## 9: A Tribute to Grief

1) If you are currently in the beginning stages of grief, or if you have never opened yourself to processing your grief, would you hope to grow to the place where you could actually thank grief for its unrelenting refining qualities?

2) Are you willing to ask grief to cut through your fear and denial of death?

3) Are you ready to embrace your great loss and open your mind and heart to receive the possible benefits that grief brings? Write any of your reactions, hopes, doubts, resistances, questions, or responses in your journal.

4) Record the unanswered questions, fantasies, or recurring hopes that evolve as you explore the possibility of growing through your grief.

## 10: Grief and Journaling

1) How has journaling ever served you in the past? Write down any specific insights, frustrations, blocks, or breakthroughs that come to mind as you respond to this question.

2) List any drawbacks, fears, hopes, frustrations, or concerns you may experience in relating to keeping your journal as an ongoing practice.

3) Has writing out your feelings and thoughts proved to be helpful, or a disadvantage, in past times?

4) After reading this chapter, list two or three ways you possibly could enhance your journaling practice.

## 11: Grief and Community

1) Recall faces and write down the names of a few individuals (and/or animals, or in a favorite space in nature, etc.) where you felt surrounded with love and support during those heavy disoriented hours.

2) Close your eyes and invite the supportive energy that reverberates from the ways people, animals, and nature have surrounded you in the heart of your loss.

3) If you went through your grief alone and without support from any other person, write in your journal what that was like, how you managed to survive. List any significant choices or lingering outcomes that still cry out for your compassion, forgiveness, or amends.

4) Record any spiritual experiences you recall that turned the tide in your grieving process.

## 12: Grief and Contemplative Practice

1) Journal in hand, write your responses to this question: *Do I have a hard time just being still, doing nothing, waiting for the spirit of my depths to speak to me?*

2) Write in your journal two of your deepest questions or yearnings that relate to your current relationship to (or lack of) any Divine Presence.

3) Record whatever you remember about having an encounter with Divine Presence. Did it prove to be ho-hum, intriguing, meaningless, or influential?

4) Describe in your journal any time you have experienced God in a negative way. If so, write an honest letter to God and don't hold anything back. Then imagine you are God and write an honest response back to yourself.

## 13: Grief and Dream Work

1) Do you believe dreams play a significant role in human life? How, if ever, have dreams played a vital role in your life? Can you remember a childhood dream or a big dream that may have frightened you? Write those dreams in your journal.

2) If you are a person who "doesn't have dreams," after reading this chapter would you like to investigate and explore this phenomenology? Write your responses in your journal.

3) Have you experienced dreams guiding, warning, or protecting you?

4) After reading this chapter on dreams, can you imagine how dreams could guide you especially during times

of crisis, grief, change, and transition? Your response to these questions is important. Writing out your responses, reactions, and insights often surfaces and clarifies your awareness, introducing new depths of understanding.

## 14: Grief and Paranormal Experiences

1) Go to your journal and briefly list any mysterious, "weird," or marvelous events that you recall, especially those unique or subtle happenings that you may have kept secret for fear that you would be misunderstood.

2) Did a specific spirit animal, person, or mystical event suddenly come to you? How did you respond or react to those "weird" events at the time? Did they make a difference in your life? Did you choose to ignore what happened? Upon further reflection, can you imagine what that encounter was symbolically conveying to you?

3) Describe any experience you have had that you cannot understand and yet you know it was real, and you somehow know it was tremendously important.

4) Write your honest response to this statement in your journal: *You cannot think God, you can only love God.*[21]

---

21 This statement by William Johnston is in his introduction to *The Cloud of Unknowing.*

# Guidelines for Small Group Sharing

"To achieve genuine community the designated leader must lead and control as little as possible in order to encourage others to lead. In doing so, she or he must often admit weakness and risk the accusation of failing to lead."

**—M. Scott Peck** (p. 164)

Choosing to hide the most important events in our lives can leave us lonely, alienated, withdrawn, and depressed. We can develop healthy ways to express our deepest thoughts and feelings to others.

Human beings were created to belong together and to share with each other in mutual trust and benefit. Sharing our vulnerable stories in a safe small group with individuals who walk a similar path can provide powerful medicine for soul and body.

Choose to be in a group where your stories will experience safety and openness. Beware of groups where safety, open-mindedness, and confidentiality do not exist.

These simple guidelines have evolved from working with hundreds of small groups over forty years. While guidelines are never perfect, they can restore new depths of your story that you might otherwise disregard. Guidelines are not rules to follow; they exist to serve you in your reflection and personal sharing with others.

Suggested Guidelines for establishing and maintaining group sharing:

1) Select an appropriate meeting place: comfortable, personal, private. Keep meeting at the same location throughout.

2) Determine up-front the longevity of the group: for example, eight or ten sessions, and whether you will meet weekly, bi-weekly, monthly.

3) Three to eight committed people make a viable number for a small group.

4) Set a timeframe for your group sessions and commit to begin on time and end on time: an hour and a half or two hours at most.

5) Create a group roster with phone numbers and email addresses. Don't serve food or refreshments: filtered water, tea, and coffee is just fine.

6) Each group member commits to confidentiality: "Whatever's said here, stays here." At the first session, go around the circle and have each individual member commit aloud to total confidentiality.

7) Rotate the role of Group Leader each time you meet. After silent time, the Group Leader offers a brief reading (a selected paragraph, scripture, poem, letter; or a brief paragraph from this book).

8) After the brief reading, begin each group sharing time with a period of five minutes of silence. Obtain a bell or gong, sound it three times gently at the beginning and at the conclusion of your silent time.

9) If appropriate or needed, open the sharing time with one of the QUESTIONS FOR REFLECTION AND GROUP SHARING, to jumpstart group discussion.

10) Volunteer being a clock-watcher: providing equal time for every person keeps a group alive. Agree upon an average sharing time per person depending upon the number present at each given session, including three to five minutes for brief feedback from the group members, if requested by the sharing person. Appropriately alert the sharing person one minute before time (i.e., simply say "one minute remaining"). Do not use a loud kitchen timer. Wristwatch timers are quieter.

11) The sharing person may request extra time without extending the overall group time. In such cases, other group members can choose to sacrifice part of their allotted time.

12) Use *I messages* when sharing; share your story the way you see it, the way you experience it. While your truth is *your* truth, your truth is never the whole truth for anyone else.

13) Listen, listen, *listen*! Do not give advice or interrupt with spontaneous associations; let group silence offer its own confirmation of what was shared. Listening is not always a natural skill; listening can be learned and

practiced. Listening involves patience, understanding that we all grieve in our unique ways. Listening can mean holding your own feedback in abeyance, honoring the sharing partner's own conclusions. Our listening task must provide safety and freedom for the speaker to self-disclose naturally, sometimes beginning at a more superficial level, slowly moving deeper at his or her chosen pace.

14) You are not in this group to take care of or to teach others or give opinions. You are in this group to grow, learn, and share the only story you have to share—your own—and to be present to each individual who discloses his and her unique story. Your reason for being in a grief sharing group may well be as poet Mary Oliver wrote in her poem "The Journey," "to save the only life you could save."

15) The person sharing may invite brief feedback or questions after he/she finishes. Group members are never obliged to offer feedback. Most of the time silence can be the best support.

16) During the final group session, invite every group member to name: 1) a strength experienced in the group process, 2) a wished-for-behavior that may improve group sharing, 3) what you learned about yourself being in the group, 4) what you value most, and 5) how being in this sharing group has made a difference in your life.

17) Remain accountable and proactive in your attendance. If you find you cannot attend the next session, contact

someone in the group early on and explain why you will not be there so the entire group can support you in your absence.

18) Again, always begin on time and conclude on time. There will always be more opportunities for everyone who wishes to connect and share between group sessions.

19) If some individuals wish to continue beyond the eight to ten original sessions, terminate this group on the final session and set a date and place for all those who wish to continue, inviting any new members who wish to join. Set the top group number at no more than twelve for maximum sharing time.

20) Review and update these guidelines thoroughly at the beginning session of your next group, even if all the old members remain.

21) Honor good questions more than answers. Remember the words of Rilke, quoted earlier: "Be patient toward all that is unresolved within your heart . . . try to love the questions themselves. The point is to live everything. Live the questions now. Perhaps you will then gradually, without noticing it, live along some distant day into the answer."

# Condolences

*December 15, 2006*

Dear Hal and everyone on this e-mail list, I have a Betsy story I'd like to share.

Several years ago, Hal and Betsy held House Church. Growing up next door to them gave me easy access to their House Church, so I went a lot. One freaky Sunday in April it snowed something like six or seven inches. As I was making my way through all the snow in the backyard, Betsy opened up the back door and called out, "Blair, are you coming to House Church?"

"House Church isn't canceled?" I shot back.

"No way!" Betsy said.

Three weeks ago, when Betsy was in very bad shape in the hospital, I dreamed I was in my family room of that old house. Betsy appeared at the back door. I hugged her and said I was happy she was feeling better. I don't remember exactly what she said but it was something to the effect of, "It isn't over yet and there is still more work to do." She felt so soft when I hugged her; I remember that part of the dream vividly. The thing most remarkable in the dream was the fact that Betsy had all this snow in her hair and on her shoulders.

I didn't consider these two events together until the day after Betsy died. As we all know, it snowed like mad just a few hours after she passed. The next morning, at 5:00 A.M., I was in my driveway about to go to work and I had to stop and pause for the beauty.

Everything was white. I could not get over how still everything was . . . and quiet! It was so amazingly quiet. I stood there absorbing such quiet beauty. And I thought about another quiet beauty—Betsy.

It was then I recalled having my dream. Followed by the memory of her on that strange snowy April so many years ago. I had this intense feeling I did not know how to say goodbye. Just then, I kid you not, a great flash in the sky lit up everything like a 50-million-watt light bulb and a second later a bone-humming thunder clap!

Betsy, my snowy lady, I'll consider that *hello*!

Blair Cooke

❋

*December 20, 2006*

Dear Hal,

You have been in my prayers and thoughts since I became aware of Betsy's illness. I have often projected myself into the space where you were and tried to send caring thoughts your way. I found the space you now occupy strangely comforting when I was alone and while my years of deep grieving were soul tested. Those years resulted in my capacity to continue to live my life to the fullest and have a deeper faith in a life that goes on beyond the world we know. I believe I can comprehend where you are now. Have a good, deep mourning for the love of your life. Rest assured Betsy is well and cares so much for you in a dimension we cannot even begin to fathom.

Take care,

Howard Morgan

✳

*December 11, 2006*

Hal,

Thank you for understanding where I am in my own grieving process as you courageously share quite openly what you are going through in your early stages of grieving. What you are writing is too much for me to bear at this particular time of my own grief. For now, please take me off your list because your emails surface too much pain relating to my own loss. Maybe later.

Yes, I do trust that it gets much more bearable as time goes on. The pain isn't as fresh now as it was. I hope someday to move beyond this into more objectivity and acceptance.

I will hang on, dear friend. I shall stay with my feelings and do what I need to do. As you said, we all grieve in our own ways, and there isn't a right or wrong way. I plan to see you after the holidays when our lives begin to mend a bit.

Blessings,

M. A.

✳

*December 28, 2006*

Dear Hal,

Thank you for including us on your mailing list. On December 18, 1986, Michael and I lost our first-born son who was born many months early. As a mother, I could not find a way to go on, and had a really tough time. Yet I figured out how to grieve and what I could do to survive with all that good old "Time," and I made it.

There are days that bring me back to that very moment when he was born, to that deep dark place I was at in those months to follow. December is still an awkward time; it's a time of joy but yet a time of that moment in our lives that changed us forever. I still miss him and wonder every day what it would be like if he were here. I am not in any way saying how it feels, because I don't; but I do know how it feels to lose a part of one's self, someone you love more than life itself, and I can only say I AM SO SORRY.

All our love,

Mike & Kim Husko

# Acknowledgments

My deep, heartfelt gratitude to you, Jill, my wife, for your unfailing love and support throughout this project. Eight years after Betsy's death, we were married. Second marriages, as so many people know, are no small undertaking, including the merging and reorientation of relationships, memories, traditions, locations, furniture, energy patterns, and families. Jill, you will never take Betsy's place and she will never take your place. My love for Betsy and my love for you have evolved into a seamless, ongoing dynamic of mutual growth, benefit, and trust. To have written this book alongside you, with your quiet support and wise encouragement, has proved to be a sheer grace and amazingly therapeutic for both of us. Thank you, precious friend.

I belong to four wonderful children (Lib, Rachel, Sam, and Joanna) and ten grandchildren (Mirabai, who is now with Betsy; Sarasvati, Andrea, Sammy, Alice, Betsy, Emily, Raina, Yeager, and Jessie). I am consistently sustained by all your unique voices, forthright opinions, and a breathtaking variety of differences that enliven my elder years. You have lightened my load and enlightened my life; you have exhibited tremendous compassion and continuity. You kept showing up; you held me so tenderly during those impossibly stressful days prior to and following Betsy's death. You surrounded me and believed in me during our challenging times of grief and, later, adjusting to the radical changes created by my new life with Jill. I shall remain grateful to you all as we continually grow, play, learn, and share together.

Megan Wells, nationally renowned master storyteller and word magician, I thank you for wondrously transforming sixteen hundred pages of grieving mishmash from my notes, journals, emails, and reflections. You skillfully reached into the core of my experience, edited, and magically moved this material into a manageable story narrative format. This book would not exist without your genius and personal care.

Cathy Pezdirtz, well done! You are a gifted author, publisher, and an eagle-eyed editor; you remain Betsy's lifelong spiritual companion and someone very dear to me and to my family. I can easily imagine that Betsy is very proud of you!

I did not walk alone through those grieving years. I was surrounded. Many people stepped forward and encircled our entire family during those dark months. You know who you are. You were there. Many of you spent the night at the hospital when I was too exhausted. Betsy was never left alone, day or night. You held us in your circles of compassion through so many practical and simple acts. Together, we have created a legacy of healing love, stability, and lifelong companionships. Without each of you and your timely touches, this story would have been radically different. Thank you for permission to quote several of you.

Martin Rowe, you did not give up on me! I have profound gratitude for your mentoring and for giving me this opportunity to publish with Lantern Books. René Gorbold: thank you for gifting us all with your extraordinary quilting expertise. Scott Kafora: great job on the book cover. Bob Shallenberg, Tom Witt, and Alan Levin: hats off to your professional photo work. I owe a great debt of gratitude to you who took the time and energy to read and endorse my manuscript, squeezing it into three sentences, and opening up its potential to prospective readers.

I will never find the words to fully express my most profound gratitude for Dean and Lois Griffith and Ben Johnson, who found me in Southern California and invited Betsy and me and my young family to Chicago in 1968, setting the stage for all that has been described in this book. Looking back over half a century in Chicagoland, I am drawn to a quote by Dr. Sam Shoemaker who mentored me as a young man: "It's been a great journey. I would not have missed it for anything."

Finally, I am deeply indebted to Winston, our four-legged, one-eyed Shih-Tzu, who faithfully remains close by my side as I write, making darn sure this octogenarian does not forget to play ball and get him outside to baptize his favorite places on our daily around-the-block walks.

—*Hal Edwards*

# Bibliography

Anonymous. *The Cloud of Unknowing: and The Book of Privy Counseling*, ed. William Johnston (New York: Doubleday, 1973).

Anonymous. *The Way of a Pilgrim, and The Pilgrim Continues*, tr. R. M. French (Pasadena, CA: Hope Publishing, 1993).

Becker, Ernest. *The Denial of Death* (New York: Free Press, 1973).

Bellg, Laurin, MD. *Near Death in the ICU: Stories from Patients Near Death and Why We Should Listen to Them* (Appleton, WI: Sloan Press, 2016).

Didion, Joan. *The Year of Magical Thinking* (New York: Vintage, 2006).

Dugan, Irene, and Avis Clendenen. *Love Is All Around in Disguise: Meditations for Spiritual Seekers*. Asheville, NC: Chiron Publications, 2004).

Frank, Anne. *Anne Frank: The Diary of a Young Girl* (New York: Bantam Reissue, 1993).

Gawande, Atul. *Being Mortal: Medicine and What Matters in the End* (New York: Henry Holt, 2014).

Gibran, Kahlil, *The Prophet*, "On Joy and Sorrow" (New York: Alfred A. Knopf, 1923).

Goldberg, Natalie. *Writing Down the Bones: Freeing the Writer Within* (Boston: Shambhala, 1986).

Haas, Peter Traben. *Centering Prayers: A One-Year Companion for Going Deeper into the Love of God* (Brewster, MA: Paraclete, 2007).

Higgins, Michael W. *Thomas Merton: Faithful Visionary* (Collegeville, MN: Liturgical Press, 2014).

Keating, Thomas. *Open Mind, Open Heart: 20th Anniversary Edition*. New York: Continuum, 2006).

Keating, Thomas, and Joseph Boyle (with Lucette Verboven). *World without End*. New York: Bloomsbury, 2017).

Kelsey, Morton T. *Afterlife: The Other Side of Dying* (New York: Crossroad, 1982).

Kirk, Russ, ed. *Death Poems: Classic, Contemporary, Witty, Serious, Tear-Jerking, Wise, Profound, Angry, Funny, Spiritual, Atheistic, Uncertain, Personal, Political, Mythic, Earthy, and Only Occasionally Morbid* (San Francisco: Disinformation, 2013).

Kübler-Ross, Elisabeth. *On Death and Dying: What the Dying Have to Teach Doctors, Nurses, Clergy and Their Own Families* (New York: Scribner, 2014).

Kübler-Ross, Elisabeth, and David Kessler. *Life Lessons: Two Experts on Death & Dying Teach Us about the Mysteries of Life & Living* (New York: Scribner, 2000).

Lewis, C. S. *A Grief Observed* (New York: HarperCollins, 1994).

——. *Surprised by Joy: The Shape of My Early Life* (New York: HarperCollins, 1955/1994).

Lindbergh, Anne Morrow. *Gift from the Sea: 50th Anniversary Edition* (New York: Pantheon, 2005).

Luke, Helen. *Old Age: Journey into Simplicity* (Great Barrington, MA: Lindisfarne, 2010).

Merton, Thomas. *The Seven Storey Mountain: An Autobiography of Faith* (New York: Mariner, 1999).

Mitford, Jessica. *The American Way of Death* (New York: Simon & Schuster, 1963).

Moody, Raymond. *Life After Life* (New York: Bantam, 1976).

Moore, Thomas. *Ageless Soul: The Lifelong Journey toward Meaning and Joy* (New York: St. Martin's, 2017).

Neihardt, John G. *Black Elk Speaks: Being the Life Story of a Holy Man of the Oglala Sioux*, Premier Edition (Albany: State University of New York Press, 2008).

Nepo, Mark. *The Book of Awakening: Having the Life You Want by Being Present to the Life You Have* (San Francisco: Conari, 2011).

Peck, M. Scott. *The Different Drum: Community Making and Peace* (New York: Simon & Schuster, 1987).

Rilke, Rainer Maria. *Letters to a Young Poet*, tr. M. D. Herter Norton (New York: Norton, 1934).

Rinpoche, Sogyal. *The Tibetan Book of Living and Dying* (San Francisco: HarperSanFrancisco, 1993).

Rohr, Richard. *Falling Upward: A Spirituality for the Two Halves of Life* (San Francisco: Jossey-Bass, 2011).

Wilber, Ken. *Grace and Grit: Spirituality and Healing in the Life and Death of Treya Killam Wilber* (Boston: Shambhala, 1993).

Yungblut, John. *On Hallowing One's Diminishments*. Pamphlet 292 (Wallingford, PA: Pendle Hill, 1990).


*Active Imagination*

Hannah, Barbara. *Encounters with the Soul: Active Imagination* (Santa Monica, CA: Sigo Press, 1981).

Johnson, Robert A. *Inner Work* (New York: HarperCollins, 1986).

———. *Owning Your Own Shadow* (New York: HarperCollins, 1991).

Kelsey, Morton. T. *The Other Side of Silence* (Mahwah, NJ: Paulist Press, 1976).

von Franz, Marie-Louise. *Alchemical Active Imagination* (Shambhala: Boston, 1997).

# About the Author

**HAL L. EDWARDS** has worked for more than half a century as a clergyman, marketplace coach, pastoral psychotherapist, and spiritual director. An ordained United Methodist pastor, he served local parishes in North Carolina, Kentucky, Minnesota, and Southern California before becoming President of Christian Laity of Chicago, where he served for almost three decades. During his decade as President of CityQuest, he facilitated conferences, workshops, and home gatherings for people who represent many of the world's major religions. Hal lives with his wife, Jill, in Wauconda, Illinois. He is a father of four children and grandfather of ten.

# About the Publisher

LANTERN BOOKS was founded in 1999 on the principle of living with a greater depth and commitment to the preservation of the natural world. In addition to publishing books on animal advocacy, veganism, religion, and environmentalism, Lantern is dedicated to printing books in the United States on recycled paper and saving resources in day-to-day operations. Lantern is honored to be a recipient of the highest standard in environmentally responsible publishing from the Green Press Initiative.